John Schubert has written more than just another "how-to" book on running. It's a "why-to" and "why-to-keep-on" book, and these are deeper subjects that motivate far better than any compendium of basic advice.

—Amby Burfoot, former Boston Marathon winner and Executive Editor *Runner's World* magazine

---

Schubert's enthusiasm for running is contagious; for the beginner he shows how improving fitness and performance can be much more fun than drudgery.

—Ed Ayres, Founding Editor and Publisher, *Running Times* magazine

D1304600

CYCLING
by Arlene Plevin
HIKING
by Cindy Ross
SAILING
by Michael B. McPhee

Forthcoming

CLIMBING

CROSS-COUNTRY SKIING

SCUBA DIVING

SKIING

RUNNING

A CELEBRATION OF THE SPORT AND
THE WORLD'S BEST PLACES TO ENJOY IT

———————

by JOHN SCHUBERT

Illustrations by Jim Deal

Travel section by
Lydia Chang and Peter Oliver

———————

A RICHARD BALLANTINE/BYRON PREISS BOOK

To my memories of the 1969 Cate track team, and eight wonderful Cate and Swarthmore cross-country teams; to coaches Elliott S. Andrews, Clement Joe Stefanowicz and Sandy Smith, and trainer Doug Weiss; and to hundreds of supportive teammates and worthy competitors. (Lyle, Ben, and Jock, where are you?) Thanks, guys, for what you did for me. Thanks more than words can say.

John Schubert, a distance runner since 1967, was co-captain of the Swarthmore College cross country team and has been ranked 230th nationally among U.S. marathoners with a 2:36 marathon.

"Over the years, I've sampled all sorts of exercise and recreation, from running to bike racing to white water kayaking to flying an airplane upside down," he said. "Despite this bounty of choice, I continue to find running genuinely exciting. The other sports allow one to see the world, but running, much more than any of them, has made me see more of myself. More than any other sport, running has defined what I am today."

Schubert, a technical writer and marketing consultant, is also a well-known writer in the sport of bicycling.

Running: A Celebration of the Sport and the World's Best Places to Enjoy It

Series Editor: Richard Ballantine
Design Director: Byron Preiss
Editor: Babette Lefrak
Associate Editor: Brendan Healey
Contributors: Peter Oliver
Designer: Stephen Brenninkmeyer and Nancy Novick
Cover Design: Fabrizio La Rocca
Cover Photograph: Jim Devault/Tony Stone Worldwide
Cover Illustrator: Marco Marinucci

Special thanks to Kristina Peterson, Publisher of Fodor's; Michael Spring, Editorial Director of Fodor's; Basil Honikman of TACSTATS/USA; Pete Cava of The Athletics Congress; Dan Brannen, TAC Ultrarunning subcommittee chairman; the New York Road Runners Club, John Lucas, Dr. David Newman, Nin Chi, Kathy Huck, Nellie Kurtzman, Jessica Steinberg.

Special Sales
Fodor's Travel Publications are available at special discounts for bulk purchases (100 copies or more) for sales promotions or premiums. Special editions, including personalized covers, excerpts of existing guides, and corporate imprints, can be created in large quantities for special needs. For more information write to Special Marketing, Fodor's Travel Publications, 201 East 50th Street, New York, 10022. Inquiries from Canada should be sent to Random House of Canada, Ltd., Marketing Department, 1265 Aerowood Drive, Mississauga, Ontario L4W 1B9. Inquiries from the United Kingdom should be sent to Fodor's Travel Publications, 20 Vauxhall Bridge Road, London, England, SWIV 2SA.

MANUFACTURED IN THE UNITED STATES OF AMERICA.
10 9 8 7 6 5 4 3 2 1

Acknowledgments

Runners love to share their sport, and hundreds have shared their knowledge with me over the years. This book's information and inspiration came from countless sources. Thanks to all, and especially to the following:

Several Swarthmore college friends and teammates wrote and phoned me with input for this book. Many thanks to Tom Crochunis, Rick Schultz, Nanette Bertaut, coach Joe Stefanowicz, and especially John Devlin (who once held the record for the JFK 50-mile run). Two other coaches, Sandy Smith and Elliott Andrews, gave me the knowledge and inspiration to love this sport, as did trainer Doug Weiss. Teammate Dave Johnson and freelance coach Art Hindle, the sport's two most analytical fans, were great teachers. My neighbors, Rob and Kevin Sanford, told me yes, I could do it.

Thanks to Dave Sellers, for sharing his running library. Thanks to Anne M.K. Schubert, my physical therapist and (usually) patient wife, for lending her technical expertise.

Thanks to other writers for early inspiration: Hal Higdon, Joe Henderson, Bob Anderson, and doctors Gabe Mirkin and George Sheehan. Pioneering exercise physiologists Peter Cavanaugh, David Costill, and Ed Burke greatly aided my understanding of this deceptively complex activity.

Thanks to the team managers, equipment caretakers, and other unsung heroes who make the sport happen.

CONTENTS

SPORT FOR LIFE

A RUNNER'S GUIDE TO 25 GREAT CITIES OF THE WORLD

INTRODUCTION

It's a quiet, snowy night. The road is coated with an inch of snow, a perfect consistency that offers just enough traction for my running shoes. No fool is out driving in this weather, but I'm bounding down a country road, enjoying the view. A guy on a small motorbike appears, having just as much fun as I am. We stop and exchange greetings. We both say the same thing at once: "People inside don't know what they're missing!"

It's a pleasant evening. Three Siberian huskies come bounding around a trail in the woods. Heads down, ears back, straining at their harnesses, they charge up a long, steep hill. The cool twilight air invigorates them. They are natural connoisseurs of the joys of long-distance running, and this hill just makes them run faster. I'm running with them, sharing the joy of their romp. Unbeknownst to them, I'm also elated by the news from my stopwatch: on this, our private cross-country course, we are about to set a new world's record. The split time at the top of the hill is half a minute ahead of record pace.

It's about 100 degrees. Not a single blade of grass grows on the five-acre barren plateau; the outline of the quarter-mile track is shown by lines of lime. The two-mile race starts, the runners moving out as fast as in a quarter-mile dash, but I don't take the bait.

1

I stick to the more modest pace I can maintain. After one lap, I'm in fifth place. One by one, the rabbits drop off the impossible pace they'd set for themselves until only one superb athlete remains ahead. Halfway through the race, Jock Collins (who was also a national-caliber downhill skier) is 100 yards ahead. But even he wilts in this heat. On the seventh lap, I catch and pass him. My coach looks at his stopwatch and screams, "Schubert, if you want that school record, now go!" On the final lap, I put 100 yards between myself and Collins, and yes, I break the school record. (Okay, it was a slow 10:57, if you must know. But it was fun, and for me it was fast.) Collins's coach walks over to congratulate me.

Exercise. Elation. Bragging rights. Release and relaxation. Calmness and a feeling of accomplishment. The feeling of boundless energy and strength. Health.

Running has all these qualities, but the most important, the one I want most of all to share with you, is the elation. As well as providing a route to improved self-esteem, reduced stress, and a fountain of youth, the simple, unprepossessing sport of running can be loads of fun.

It pains me to see runners who are slow and labored, who are grimly bettering themselves, who have no concept of enjoying the sport. They're missing so much. I thought running was the activity from hell when I first tried it. Then, by an unlikely series of lucky accidents, I learned how this sweaty, grunting, injury-prone sport could elate me like no other.

I'd like to shorten that learning process for you, and take the luck out of it. You deserve to have all the fun I had, and you might as well learn every lesson the easy way.

This is not a traditional how-to book, although I hope you'll learn useful information here. Rather, it's a "why" book, an appreciation book, a "learn from my mistakes" book, and an attempt to give you the benefit of my quarter century of running experience. Above all, I hope I've made the beauty of the sport more accessible.

—*John Schubert*

BEGINNINGS

John Schubert, age 14. P.E. class. A waste of my precious time.

Basketball, baseball, whatever they're playing, I'm bad at it. When I try to practice and improve, the results are so discouraging I give up. If you aren't born with lots of fast-twitch muscle fiber and good hand-eye coordination, you can't do much to improve your skills at these sports.

On the field, the other kids shove me out of the way so they can play. I just stand on the sidelines, bored, waiting for the game to end. When the captains pick their teams, I always get picked last.

John Schubert, age 16.

It's commencement at school, and they're handing out trophies to outstanding students. I stand proudly when I'm given the award for "Most Inspirational Athlete." All the lacrosse and basketball stars and all the graduating seniors were bypassed for that honor. I had become school record holder and conference champion in the two-mile, and no one believed I did it easily. A year later, I would break a 36-year-old school record for the mile. Perhaps most important, I had respect from others.

Yep, it's the same John Schubert in both stories.

The difference between the stories is running—at my own pace, in my own time. Each footstep gave its own feeling of accomplishment and trained my body so the next step was a bit faster and bouncier.

As a route to personal improvement, no sport is simpler or easier than running. Genetic inheritance does make some runners faster than others, but every runner can gain satisfaction from attaining personal goals.

The discovery that you can improve through your own efforts can occur at any age. I was lucky it happened to me when I was relatively young. But you don't have to be young to take up running. My brother waited until he was 39 before he started running, and yet, the improvement in his health and outlook was wonderful. Many other people have had similar transformations when they were much older.

If you're out of shape, you're not too old to change that fact. Believe it.

If you're not a "natural athlete," as defined by sports with bats and balls and nets, running can show you abilities you didn't know you had.

A few weeks before I sat down to write this book, I chanced to have my baseball swing analyzed by computer. I'm just as crummy as I was 30 years ago: I can swing the bat tip at only 26 miles per hour—half the speed of a good high school player, a third the speed of a major league player. By the standards of sports with bats and balls and nets, that would consign me to being a hard-core deskbound nonathlete. But what do they know? I run actively, I take my children on hikes and bike rides, I have a resting pulse around 50, and acquaintances assume I'm about 10 years younger than I really am.

I owe it all to running—not because running is my only sport (it most certainly is not) but because running opened the doors for me. It was through running that I learned to enjoy exercise and the out-of-doors, that I found a skinny weak kid could bring home first-place ribbons, that I earned greater respect from both myself and from other people. These factors emboldened me to try and enjoy other activities (not including baseball!). I've been an Outward Bound instructor, a canoeist and kayaker, a bicycle racer, and tourist (which I regularly write about for *BikeReport* magazine, and in my other books). I have a clear vision of how to help my children enjoy these kinds of activities.

Every runner has stories of how she or he found this sport. I marvel at how lucky the stories often are: a challenge, a dare, a lecture from the doctor, or some other such event makes couch potatoes try an activity they expect to detest, and then learn to love.

My lucky break came after I'd been transferred to a new school with a new physical education program, on the day Coach Draeger announced we'd be "doing" track for a few weeks. That day's assignment: run one mile.

Now I'd heard of people running a mile. At the time, Jim Ryun's exploits as a world-record miler were the stuff of *LIFE* magazine articles. I had read those articles and marveled at the novelty of someone actually running a whole mile—in competition, no less. But me? I could never do that.

Coach Draeger had us run a half mile, walk a

quarter mile, then run another half mile. I did that. It hurt. And was I sore for days after.

So it went for several weeks. My body adapted to the running, and the hurt lessened. I actually liked running a little bit; it was the first time in my life that P.E. was anything other than a gross waste of time.

At the end of the school year, all the students had a series of fitness tests. For me, the results were typically humiliating. Broad jumps, sprints, and other such events all put me in the bottom 25 percent. In the softball throw, I scored in the fifth percentile for the *girls!* (This was back when a boy was allowed to acknowledge such a male chauvinist yardstick.)

Then came the 600-yard time trial. I actually beat some of the big strong boys. I was better than the 50th percentile—an honor I usually enjoyed only in the confines of math class. My time, if faint memory is correct, was 1:49 (a 5:20-mile pace). Not bad for a skinny kid.

Today, in the enlightened 1990s, a kid who can run a little might be encouraged to run three or four times a week for fitness and, if he continued to get faster, sample a few local races. But when I was a kid, the only next step was the track team, and that was too much of a step up. I wasn't *that* fast. And the team didn't need warm bodies desperately enough to recruit someone like me.

Well, I wound up on a track team anyway. It was after another transfer to another school, a bizarre new set of P.E. requirements, and a Hobson's choice between track or the hated sports with balls and nets.

Can You Be a Contender?

Do you have the talent to be a world-class long-distance runner? Running is the sport where desire counts more than talent, and my limited successes show that. But for high-level competition, top runners are both born and made.

How do I know this? Long-distance performance does depend on short-distance performance. Good performances in shorter races show you have the supremely efficient biomechanics to run a 2:09 marathon.

Scratch a world-class marathon runner, and you'll usually find a 4:10 or 4:15 mile on his race resume, and a 4:25 or better during high school. Those mile times, in turn, predict that the runner can do a 400-meter time below 53 seconds, and a 100-yard dash of 11.0 or better. Since I could not break 12.5 for 100 yards, I was a mediocre college miler (4:33). Thus I wasn't surprised when I didn't break 2:30 for the marathon.

Of course, there are exceptions to these observations. Some people do make it to the top ranks with less innate talent than others. But the odds are against them.

I could run hard, puke my guts out, and come in last, or join the baseball team and stand around bored.

I joined the track team, where I was assigned the 660-yard dash (a weird distance, but this was in Southern California).

It was not a nurturing environment. I was still a skinny kid learning to jog, and the expectation that I would try to run, and run fast, was intimidating.

The races were hell and humiliation. I was second to last in my first 660, a rout against junior high school students several years younger than myself. In the next race I was fifth (probably out of six). Then I was dead last.

None of this convinced me I had any future as an athlete.

Then one day, we hopped on the bus and rode to a three-way meet. Only two people had entered the two-mile, and the scoring gave points for four places. Coach Sandy Smith drafted me to run the longer race: "John, you can't come in any lower than third. You'll score points."

I didn't think of myself as a two-miler, and it seemed like a cheap way to score points. But I couldn't very well say no.

My finishing time is engraved in my brain: 12:46.6. (Those old mechanical stopwatches were never accurate to 0.1 second for an event that long, but we'll just let that pass.) I was third. But the surprise of the day was that I *didn't* get lapped by our school's star two-miler.

There is a difference between short, fast races and

the long races. Natural talent—the kind you're born
with or you're not—is important for short races.
Long races require training and desire. If you want
to prevail in the longer distances, the first requirement
is that you want to prevail more than the next guy
wants to.

In other words, you gotta be dogged. I am.

The two-mile and I became fast friends. In the
next race, I placed fourth and actually lapped two
runners. The next race was the season finale, the
league championship. I took home fifth place, a
yellow ribbon, the knowledge that I'd beaten four
other runners, and a time of 12:06.

That yellow ribbon was a turning point—all the
proof I needed that being determined would get results.

The following two years, I ran cross-country and
track. I won lots of races. I improved greatly, enough
to say, with a straight face, that I wanted to run
college cross-country. (Boy, I wished I could rub that
in the noses of those kids who lorded their baseball
skills over me.)

Running in college continued the storybook
success of high school, but only after an intimidating
beginning. My freshman year, the team's second-best
runner was a candidate for the Olympic marathon
(he was ranked about 10th among U.S. marathoners,
and had finished as high as 18th in the Boston
Marathon), and the rest of the top seven were no
slouches either. Yet after one and a half seasons in
college, I clawed my way onto the lower rungs of the
varsity. My senior year, I was co-captain. I didn't

attain the lofty heights of my friends who got Olympic feelers, but the rewards I did get were wonderful. What a blast those races were! Five miles of thrashing through the woods at speeds approaching 5:15 per mile (on a good day).

Thanks to running, I was empowered, elated, and thrilled. My personality was altered for the better, by the infusion of self-confidence, the excitement of racing well, and the euphoria of running.

Today I seldom compete, and never race seriously. I run regularly, albeit slower than I used to. My three dogs and I look for deer and foxes as we patrol our regular trail through the woods. Every year I go through cycles: some months I train so that I'm fleet and fit; other months I can barely stagger through three miles.

Physiologically, I should be able to run as fast as ever. I'm not so old that I'd have to be slower. But neither my temperament nor my time commitments make speed a high-priority goal now. So, rather than having a past loom over me like an example I can't live up to, I use its lessons to enjoy more fully the running I do now.

This book is about being at peace with a great sport, whether your highest ambitions are ahead of you or behind you (and, indeed, whether or not you *have* any high ambitions as a runner). Whether you plod slowly and smell the flowers, or mow down national-class skiers in quest of records, you can enjoy running for its own sake.

Not so many years ago, running had no social status, no wealthy athletes, no race prizes, no nylon shorts, and no women. Knowledge of exercise physiology was passed down hand to mouth and consisted largely of incorrect myths. The Boston Marathon drew about 300 runners; a big local race might draw 50. Race fields of 15 or 20 were not unheard of. Entry fees were a dollar or two. Shoes were crummy, guaranteeing that only the few runners with the best natural stride would be able to avoid injuries. *Runner's World* magazine was an upstart publication launched from Manhattan, Kansas, and was refreshingly devoid of status consciousness or the makeup artists who work on its cover models today.

None of this stopped runners from loving their sport, and the relatively primitive conditions had less effect than you might think on the quality of the competition. It was 1969 when Derek Clayton ran the world's first 2:08 marathon.

But the gestalt of running is more important than performance. By looking at the sport when it was fresh, and devoid of commercial trappings or social standing, we gain a better appreciation for the timeless elements that make running desirable today.

One way of pondering the question, What's attractive about running? is to ask, What kind of person is attracted to running? Today, there's almost no answer to that; runners number in the millions and cut across every possible boundary you could draw. But a quarter century ago, in the words of noted runner/doctor/author George Sheehan, the people

who liked running were nervous and introverted. Flamboyant people weren't attracted to a sport in which everyone wore the same drab garb (T-shirts and gray cotton shorts), and struggled with an aerobic adversary. Running was unfashionable, so you had to be inner-directed to do it.

I don't think most of the early runners understood why they liked the sport. Sure, they liked the feeling of being in shape, and they were proud of their tiny waistlines. But so much of running then was focused on competition, rather than lifetime fitness, that runners' attitudes toward their workouts were pretty serious. They worked out hard, and running often hurt.

I never heard other runners talk about the "runner's high." We talked about how working hard made us hurt. Sure, we knew a good workout could feel good, even great, but we didn't talk about it in those terms. That was tacitly understood. No one wanted to jettison his credibility by being the first to announce, "This grunting, sweating, cramping, nauseating, puking, injury-prone activity is really euphoric."

In the midst of one hard-fought race, I remember telling myself, "This will never be popular. It's just too damn much hard work." I didn't foresee the day when millions of people would "race" hour-long 10-kilometer events, smiling and chatting the entire way. In the olden days, competition was pretty hard-nosed stuff, and running didn't exist beyond the venues of competition.

Because running was unfashionable, it was pure.

Endorphins and the Mythical Buzz

Do you burrow through running books, seeking news about the "endorphin buzz"?

Endorphins, as every good weekend athlete knows, are morphine-like substances naturally secreted by the body. For about two decades, folklore has told us that aerobic exercise causes endorphin production and that the wonderful feeling known as the "runner's high" is caused by these endorphins. Sportsmedicine types have speculated that runners become physically addicted to endorphins, which explains why some fools go running in the sleet when they have flu and a throbbing injury.

Sorry to throw cold water on a great myth, but it ain't so. Endorphins aren't generated in significant quantities by aerobic exercise. The only time you get a substantial endorphin secretion is during rare events, like the proverbial story of a soldier who gets shot and doesn't know it for an hour. Endorphins are for pain avoidance in extreme conditions.

This doesn't make the runner's high any less wonderful. It just underscores how wonderful it is to fill your brain and muscles with oxygen, to smell the fresh air, and to warm up your muscles and use them. These are the real causes of the runner's high.

People who ran, or who promoted races, did so because they loved the sport. Corporate sponsorships were few and small. Shoe companies were tiny, homey versions of their present-day selves.

The purity and lack of fashionability led to a sense of intense camaraderie among runners. Part of that camaraderie came from having to put up with the ridicule of people who didn't know running could feel good. Part came from the shared excitement of having conquered personal Everests. Part came from the mutual respect among people who work hard at something. Part came from the compatibility of people independent enough to seek out an activity so unfashionable.

And there was that shared secret, that no one dared say out loud: *This feels good!*

The stereotype of the 1960s lonely runner and his inability to articulate the sport's pleasures, masked one of running's essential charms: you could be left alone to enjoy it. Running by oneself could be a private pleasure. Running with others, we shared the tacit acknowledgement that this was gobs of fun.

Because there was no hope of being fashionable, runners made no concession to fashion. Often, that meant no more than wearing those drab-colored cotton shorts, but it also meant we didn't have to please anyone or live up to the expectations of people who didn't understand the sport.

I liked it that way. I preferred races with no spectators. All I wanted was a well-marked path through the woods, 30 other people, and a guy with a clipboard and a stopwatch. Usually, that's exactly what I got.

Sometimes, well-meaning athletic departments would "give" us spectators by scheduling cross-country races to coincide with halftime at football games. Football crowds cheer at anything that shows off bare legs, so I wasn't overly flattered by their attention. And the spectators unintentionally imposed demands on us. Look nice. Smile and wave. Those are bigger demands than they might seem. Runners often turn inward before a race, focusing their mental energy. There's a long warm-up and lots of stretching to be done. At such times it can take enormous effort to act gracious, to distract oneself from pre-race preparations, just to exchange blandishments with people who thought you were a nutty sideshow to the football game.

Most times, however, we didn't have to please anyone for any reason, because no one gave a damn about what we were doing anyway. Runners had the luxury of being left alone.

Running wasn't a fad. There was no element of its being the thing to do. It was kind of working class, egalitarian. Blue-collar workers and educated professionals looked exactly the same in those T-shirts. The best marathon runner in Philadelphia was a black construction worker named Moses Mayfield. He was faster than almost any of the banker/triathlete types of today. Are people like Moses welcomed in today's white-collar fields of runners? I hope so, but sometimes fear not.

Ed Ayres, who was the founding editor and publisher of *Running Times Magazine,* typified the attitude of the times in the title of a magazine article he wrote in 1966: "What are you running in your underwear for?" That was a typical reaction bystanders had when they saw Ed training. (He was a leading U.S. marathon runner at the time.)

Before the boom, there was almost no running equipment available. Cold weather meant improvising on the clothing front, because conventional sweatpants were (and are) horribly bulky; they restrict your motion too much. (To this day, I prefer to wear the cheap long johns I learned to use back then.) Shoes were okay for grassy surfaces, but had neither cushioning for running on pavement nor sole tread for slippery surfaces. An accurate stopwatch with a multijewel movement was an elite treat, worth a couple hundred bucks in today's dollars. (The cheap stopwatches of the time, with only one jewel in the movement, just couldn't be calibrated accurately.)

The running community was small enough that you could feel like you were a significant part of it, even nationally. Since it was based around high school and college running, there was a strong sense of shared experience—something that was diffused by demographic diversity and sheer numbers in later years, when millions of new recruits of all ages took up the sport.

Two magazines, *Runner's World* and *Long Distance Log,* were published in the 1960s. They were slim, crude, and delightfully unpretentious. And they

The Blue-Collar Advantage

You who do physical work for a living—pounding nails, carrying mail, building things—probably don't feel much like running when you get home from work.

But you have a major leg up on pencil-pushing yuppies. Your heart and lungs are in training all the time. Theirs are sedentary all day long.

So, with that fitness base, you can use relatively little training to hone your running. Take, for example, my old teammate John Devlin. In 1980, when he was 26 and running a lawn-mowing company, he ran 700 practice miles. Not much. The following year, he ran 1,400 miles—still not much (that's 27 miles per week). Yet during those two years he ran a 70-minute 10-miler, a 2:36 marathon, won a cross-country race, and did well in many other events.

John's strategy: he ran only when he wasn't mowing. That meant weekends and days of bad weather. He used his physical labor as his fitness base and did hard high-quality training for his limited running mileage.

printed your name in their innumerable listings if you placed in a race. For some years, *Runner's World* printed a separate book listing every marathoner in the country under three hours. You could sit down and count all the names ahead of yours to determine your national ranking (in 1973, mine was 230). It made you feel like you were really part of something.

Even though the world-record performances were reasonably fast by today's standards, it was much easier for an ordinary runner to feel close to the elite levels. For example, in 1972, a runner could qualify for the U.S. Olympic Trials marathon by running 2:30 (5:43 per mile). That's not exactly easy, but as one writer observed, it was attainable by runners with a lot of heart and not that much talent. If you were pretty good but not really Olympic material, the trials were still something you could attain. (That didn't last; by 1976, the standard had been raised to 2:23, allowing only those with great heart and great talent to attend.)

Some other prestigious events were also more accessible to ordinary runners back then. Shortly after I ran a 2:53 marathon, my best at the time, I was invited to the national 50-kilometer championships. (That's 31 miles, and at the time I was actually tempted to attempt it.)

But there were grave drawbacks to running in the preboom era. The worst drawback was that the pleasures of running *were* a secret, and so few got to share them.

Women were almost completely excluded. In the schools and colleges that nurtured this tiny sport,

almost no women's teams existed. And what woman would want to endure the gnawing unease of being the first—not just the first on your block, but the first woman in the whole damn county—to go outside, running in long johns? What woman would want to endure the jeers and catcalls of men who couldn't imagine these women weren't running for the purpose of entertaining others?

The crummy shoes and lack of sportsmedicine knowledge caused lots of injuries. Everyone made the same painful mistakes and learned the hard way. Many of us were almost sheepish about our love of running.

I admit to occasional nostalgia for the "good old days" of running. But in my rare moments of rational thought, I know how much I'd detest them if I could get them back.

For example, earlier this year I got a mysterious knee injury—my first ever, by the way. In the good old days, that injury could well have sidelined me for life. Now, however, I have access to reams of state-of-the-art studies on runners' knees (which tell me that simple stretching, of all things, is the most likely cure for that injury). I was able to have my knee X-rayed and reviewed by an expert orthopedic surgeon, who is a fine athlete himself. I'm reasonably secure in the knowledge that if the knee did require surgery, I could count on a state-of-the-art arthroscopy job, which would have me back running in a month.

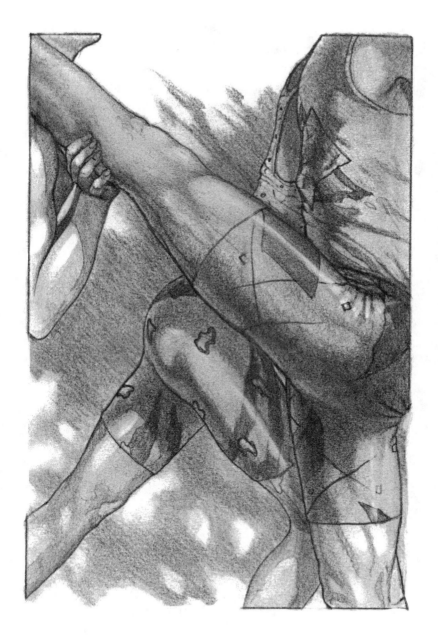

The most dangerous part of the surgery would be the drive to the hospital.

None of these things was possible in the cotton T-shirt era. Information about running injuries was nearly nonexistent. The best surgical techniques would sideline you for months, and many surgeons didn't know the best techniques.

Rumors, misinformation, and myths have been burned and buried, as running's information network has grown in quality and size.

Another example: thanks to Dr. Gabe Mirkin, author of *The Sportsmedicine Book,* all runners can know how to prevent shin splints; we stretch our calf muscles, so we don't have excess muscle imbalance between the calves and the shins. I remember, in 1970, believing that jogging on grass was a shin splint cure, and that the undefined evils of running on pavement caused that particular agony. In hindsight, it seems like pure superstition.

A high level of expertise in sportsmedicine is available everywhere—all you need is a bookstore or a magazine subscription. Knowledgeable coaches, trainers, and medical professionals are numerous.

The running shoes of old were fine . . . for lightweight runners who didn't overpronate or need traction on slippery surfaces. Today, running shoes are designed for every biomechanical niche there is. Heavy runners, light runners, pronators, supinators, winter runners, summer runners—every one of you has a special shoe. Shoes now make running feasible

Your Feet Will Thank You . . .

. . . when you coat them liberally with Vaseline before a long run.

Buy the biggest jar of the stuff you can find, and use it liberally.

Without Vaseline, I find the longest run I can hope to finish without giving myself blisters is six to eight miles. (Depending on dumb luck and which shoes I'm wearing, that figure can vary.) For longer runs, a big handful squished liberally all over the foot and between the toes is a great blister vaccine. I've run blister-free marathons because I lubed my feet well.

For longer runs, there are other places that may need grease. Your nipples and your armpits are likely candidates. Back in the prenylon days of dreadful, heavy, webbed athletic supporters, I would grease my waist so it wouldn't chafe under the elastic.

Remember that long distances cause exponentially more chafing than short distances. So get the goop ready!

for most people, not just for those gifted with perfect biomechanics.

At least as important as the technical improvements in shoes, and more advanced and informed sportsmedicine, are the sociological improvements. Running is no longer the province of pioneers and loners. You need not be the solitary eccentric, the first on your block, to be a runner. You can be with friends or make new friends. You can build a well-rounded social life around running.

Running has an infrastructure that invites newcomers, supports and cajoles participants, and keeps runners motivated year after year. These incentives are open to anyone, fast or slow, fiercely competitive or inclined to stop and smell the flowers. It's a nice improvement over the time when 90 percent of running's infrastructure was devoted solely to high school and college team members.

To get these benefits, you join a running club, or at least show up for its events. (A few clubs are more limited in their focus, catering only to up-and-coming athletes, but the majority pride themselves on the breadth of their appeal.) Your local newspaper probably lists fun runs in the section that lists local events. Sporting goods stores may be good sources of information.

Neighborhood fun runs let you enjoy the company of others in a noncompetitive setting. And if you want competition, there are tons of races in most locales.

The Short Equipment List

One of the funny things about running is how disappointed some people are that they can't spend much money on it. Why else would they have invented marathons in Hawaii?

Here are two important, but often neglected, ways to spend small amounts of money on running.

• No cotton below the belt. Stand in a city park and watch the runners, and even now, in the 1990s, you'll still see plenty of those cotton gym shorts designed when Harry Truman was president. Don't buy any yourself. Instead, buy the nylon shorts with built-in briefs. They are much, much, much more comfortable and more convenient on laundry day. You can wear them over tights. Nice ones are sold in running stores; cheap-but-usable ones are sold in discount department stores.

• Keep your hair down. A simple elastic terry-cloth headband is a radical comfort improvement. In warm weather, it keeps sweat out of your eyes; in cool weather, it helps warm up your head.

It goes without saying that you should buy good shoes. That's not a place to economize.

In this era of uneasy coexistence between the sexes, women runners have somewhat better standing than they used to; they are relatively common, and they are fortunate enough to live in an era when most people understand that an unaccompanied woman isn't necessarily on the street for the sole purpose of inviting every boor to leer at her. Sexual harassment is still a problem, though. I wish more women would run, so the boors of the world would become inured to their presence. At least the process has started.

On a more positive note, running women have fantastic role models. In 1991, when the ageless Francie Larrieu Smith ran 10,000 meters in a world record 31:28 (that's a brisk 5:04 per mile), she was a few months shy of her 39th birthday. Performances like hers have all but erased the notion that women are slower than men. When you compare women's records with the number of women participating, you realize that women are closing in on men.

And the sheer numbers of runners. Boy, the numbers. So many runners are out there, and thousands of them are awfully fast.

One race tells the story: for three years (1971, 1973, 1976) I ran the Caesar Rodney Half Marathon in Wilmington, Delaware. Each time, I finished 45th. The first year, I ran 1:29 and finished 45th out of 90. The second year, I ran 1:20 and finished 45th out of 190. The third year, I ran 1:17 and finished 45th out of almost 400. In the

next few years, the race swelled to several thousand entrants. Not wanting to spoil my perfect record of 45ths, and not getting any faster either, I stopped going.

A major benefit of running today is that, while the sport and its infrastructure are huge and popular, the fad era with all its wretched excess is gone. In the maddest flush of the running boom, it seemed like everyone took up running, everyone felt obliged to appear in the hometown 10K, and almost everyone limped through a marathon, even if it took five or six painful hours. Hometown 10Ks are fine, but marathons are crummy as a fad. It's too easy to injure yourself in one.

I recall a time, with a shudder, when many people used the words *running* and *aerobic exercise* interchangeably. Swimmers and cyclists should wince at that. Hikers were unfairly maligned when the health benefits of exercise were wrongly assumed to kick in at faster speeds than hikers attain.

I love running, but I'm not going to tell you it's the perfect or the only good way to exercise. That would be an enormous disservice to people who gamely try running and simply don't like it. People should find the exercise they love. Happiness with an activity is much more important than the relatively small differences between one aerobic exercise and another.

If you choose running, you live in an era, and a society, where running is appreciated on its own terms as a lifetime sport. Most of your friends and neighbors understand and accept your running, and some of them may join you. You're not a pioneer, a social experiment, or an oddity. You're one of millions who enjoy health, camaraderie, and sometimes euphoria.

WORLD OF RUNNING

History

Running, one of the most ancient sports known to mankind, began as a utilitarian activity. The first runners ran not to lose weight but to gain weight . . . by bashing their dinner-to-be on the head with a rock.

Running is a natural activity, and races have been contested as long as people have lived, but the first formal competition may have taken place at the Tailtian Games around 1500 B.C. in northern Great Britain. The games included long- and short-distance running and are thought to have still been in existence when the Olympics began in Greece in 776 B.C.

The evidence for the existence of the Tailtian Games is scant, however, and, according to John Lucas, a professor of sport history at Penn State, "It is good history to say the Greeks invented track and field, short-distance running, and long-distance running."

Olympic runners competed in races of a few hundred yards and more than two miles. Greek women ran races in an athletic competition called the Heraea. Believed to have been held during the sixth through fourth centuries B.C., the Heraea was open only to virgin maidens.

Historians dispute the origins of the marathon, but the legendary version credits the Greek messenger Pheidippides, who ran 20 miles in 490 B.C. to deliver the message that the Greeks had defeated the Persians on the Plain of Marathon. The marathon was resurrected for the renewal of the Olympics in 1896 (a year before the first Boston Marathon), but it was only 40 kilometers, about 25 miles. The marathon took its present length in the 1908 Olympics, when the course was extended to 26 miles, 385 yards so it could start in front of Windsor Castle and finish in the Olympic Stadium.

The 1908 Olympic marathon also engendered a mild running boom in the United States when American Johnny Hayes triumphed over Italy's Dorando Pietri, who was disqualified for being helped across the finish line.

Between the classical birth of the marathon and it's twentieth-century resurgence, runners continued to compete in long-distance races. Throughout the Middle Ages, races were often held in conjunction with fairs, and running competitions flourished in eighteenth-century England with the growth of pedestrianism. "Peds," as they were called, were professional runners who competed for large amounts of money, often in long-distance races.

According to Lucas, the sport of pedestrianism migrated to the United States around 1830, but by the 1870s the emphasis was shifting to amateur competition.

Cambridge and Oxford provided the model for amateurism by establishing organized sports programs in 1857 and 1860, respectively. Their first dual meet, in 1864, was followed by the British championships in 1866 and the inauguration of the National Association of Amateur Athletes of America championships in 1879.

Cross-country began in 1837 at England's Rugby School with the Crick run. The English cross-country championships were first held in 1877. Cross-country was an Olympic event until 1924, after which it was dropped from the Olympics because it was considered too demanding for summer weather.

Training changed around World War II with the development of two new methods. Interval training is thought to have been invented in Germany in the 1930s, and fartlek "speed play" grew popular in Sweden after the war. On May 6, 1954, Roger Bannister shook the running world and broke an "unbreakable" barrier when he ran a 3-minute, 59.4-second mile in a dual meet at Oxford.

In 1956, Bill Bowerman, then Oregon track coach, was in Australia for the Olympics and saw hundreds of people running through the streets of

Melbourne. Inspired, he returned to Eugene, Oregon, and founded a road-runners club that grew to include hundreds of members.

"There was no other city in America . . . where people were doing this," Lucas said. "Bill Bowerman was the beginning of mass participation."

Bowerman's club, and others that sprang up in imitation, laid the groundwork for the road-running boom of the 1970s. Several developments helped fuel the boom. Among them was the publication of *Aerobics* by Kenneth Cooper in 1968, which promoted running as a way to better health. Frank Shorter inspired millions to hit the roads with his 1972 Olympic marathon victory. Both cause and effect of the boom were the improvements in running shoes, which made road-running less like fire walking. Jim Fixx contributed to the road-running phenomenon when he published *The Complete Book of Running,* a 1977 best-seller that elevated Fixx to gurudom.

The growth of the New York Marathon illustrates the changes in recreational running. The New York race was first held in 1970 and had only 127 starters, of whom one was a woman. After steady growth, the race nearly quadrupled in size (to 2,090 starters) in 1976 when the course changed from loops around Central Park to a tour of all five boroughs. The race continued to grow—there were 30,445 starters in the decade of the 1970s and

25,012 in 1990 alone—and potential participants now compete in lotteries for the chance to run New York.

Women's participation experienced even more exponential growth. From the lone starter of 1970, the women's contingent expanded to 5,635 starters in 1991.

Though many would argue that the running wave has crested, the effects remain. Running is no longer the province of the fast and hardy but of anyone who can lace up a pair of shoes and circle the block. □

Metric vs. English

Want to know how today's metric distances compare with the English race distances of yesteryear? Me, too.

Here's a comparison, along with an editorial comment: the recent conversion to metric race distances is silly, because it doesn't bring us the advantages of metric conversion. We don't become more competitive in world markets by making our race distances different. We do it by making our machine tools and parts interchangeable.

So here's to the old race distances, and to running them in shoes with metric spike threads:

• 100 meters is 28 feet, 1 inch longer than 100 yards. A runner doing 100 meters in 11 seconds will go through the 100-yard mark in 10.06 seconds.

• A quarter mile (440 yards) is 7 feet, 8 inches longer than 400 meters. A 50.0-second quarter-miler would hit 400 meters in 49.8 seconds.

• A half mile is 15 feet, 4 inches longer than 800 meters. A 2-minute half-miler will hit 800 meters in 1:59.5.

• 1,500 meters is 358 feet, 9 inches (119.6 yards) shy of a mile, which will give the 4:30-miler an 18.3-second advantage.

• 1,600 meters, a thoroughly silly distance contrived to imitate a mile, takes the 4:30-miler 1.6 seconds less. The mile is 30 feet, 8 inches longer.

• My favorite track distance, the 2-mile, is 717 feet, 6 inches (239.2 yards) longer than 3,000 meters. A 10-minute 2-miler hits the shorter distance in 9:19.2.

• A 5K race is 188 yards, 2 inches longer than a 3-mile. Six-minute miles (an 18:00 3-mile) will get you the longer distance in 18:38.5.

• A 10K is 376 yards, 4 inches longer than 6 miles. Those same 6-minute miles will finish the 10K in 37:17. □

Ultramarathons

It's an old aphorism that the longest journey begins with the first step, but for ultramarathoners the first step is more like a giant leap into the limits of human endurance.

These hardy athletes redefine long-distance running. For them, a marathon is just a warm-up. In a running world of tortoises and hares, they are the ultimate tortoises, slow but incredibly determined.

Although it is now practiced by a hardy few (4,000 to 5,000 active competitors in the United States), ultramarathoning was one of the most lucrative and popular sports of the late 1800s. Indoor six-day races drew large crowds to Madison Square Garden, and Charles Rowell of England won $34,000 in 1888 for winning a six-day race there. On one occasion, police had to surround Madison Square Garden to keep people from breaking into an already packed race.

The ultramarathon consists at a minimum of one continuously timed stage of more than 26.2 miles (the standard marathon length), and stretches as far as the 1,300-mile Sri Chimnoy race, the longest sanctioned race in the world, which is run every year in Flushing Meadow Park, Queens, New York.

Less than 10 percent of U.S. ultrarunners are

women, but women are competitive. In 1989, Ann Trason won the 24-hour U.S. championship, beating every man.

Various countries and regions emphasize different aspects of the sport. Western Europeans flock to 100-kilometer road runs, and multiday runs are the most popular ultramarathons in Australia and New Zealand. In South Africa, ultramarathons are more popular than marathons or 10-kilometer races.

In the United States, "ultramarathoning is primarily characterized by the phenomenon of mountain-trail running," said Dan Brannen, chairman of the Ultrarunning Subcommittee of The Athletics Congress (TAC) USA. "It's the most visible and exotic aspect of the sport in this country, and the focus is on 100-mile trail events."

The **Western States 100 Mile** is considered the preeminent U.S. ultramarathon. It's run each June from Squaw Valley, California, west-southwest over the Sierra Nevadas to Auburn, California. The course record is slightly under 16 hours, and participants who finish in less than 24 hours receive a silver belt buckle. The race is limited to 350 runners because of, as with many other trail races, safety and ecological concerns.

The **Leadville 100 Mile,** "The Race Across the Sky," is held each August. An out-and-back through the Colorado Rockies, the Leadville is the consistently highest ultramarathon course, ranging from 10,000 to 13,000 feet of elevation.

Another top U.S. ultramarathon, Utah's **Wasatch Front 100 Mile,** traverses the Wasatch Range from East Layton to Alpine each September. It is generally regarded as the most demanding of the 100-mile trail races. The route can include the highest extremes of hot and cold and particularly rough terrain.

These three, along with the **Vermont 100 Mile** in July, comprise the informal "Grand Slam" of U.S. ultrarunning, and each year about a dozen runners complete the fatiguing four.

Trail races are but one aspect of U.S. ultramarathoning. TAC also sponsors national championships in 50-kilometer, 50-mile, 100-kilometer, 100-mile, and 24-hour races on precisely measured road courses.

The 100-kilometer and the 24-hour race are the "benchmark" races of the international ultrarunning community, and the annual Ultra Distance World Cup is a 100-kilometer race. The **Del Passatore**, a 100-kilometer race through the Apennines from Florence to Faenza, Italy, and the **Biel,** a 100-kilometer run in and around Biel, Switzerland, draw thousands of runners each year.

Several 100-kilometer races, including Belgium's **Torhout** and Germany's **Rodenbach,** are beginning to offer prize money and/or expenses.

The multiday race has become the staple of ultrarunning in Australia and New Zealand, and Yiannis Kouros, a Greek in his early thirties, is dominant in that aspect of the sport. He holds every road and track record from 200 kilometers to 1,000 miles. So complete is his mastery, "He has made the sport of multiday road racing uninteresting," TAC's Brannen says.

Brannen predicts that the reintegration of South Africans into the world athletic community will revolutionize the sport. Brannen calls South Africa "the most fascinating ultranation in the world," and many top ultrarunners are South African. The 56.5-mile **Comrades Marathon** between Durban and Pietermaritzburg, which has been integrated for years, has more than 10,000 finishers.

Whether or not international ultramarathoning grows to these levels, the sport and its competitors can be counted upon, if nothing else, to be enduring. □

THE PRACTICAL RUNNER

I n the late 1970s, when the running boom was in full flower and thousands of ill-prepared runners were engaging in the dubious fad of injuring themselves in five-hour-long marathons, I often sat in New York's Central Park and watched people bettering themselves.

They sure made it look grim.

Just as eating watercress and seltzer isn't as much fun as eating ice cream and drinking a good liqueur, running on a windswept fall day isn't as much fun as sitting in a favorite bar, watching a great movie.

Or is it?

If you expect running to be grim, that certainly can be a self-fulfilling prophecy.

I have news, folks. Running can be almost hedonistic. But only if you approach it in the right spirit.

You don't have to grimace like the clench-fisted folks I used to watch in the park. You can be more like a ballroom dancer, happily going through moves you know so well.

You don't necessarily learn to enjoy running from the usual sources though. Because too often they lay a lot of pressure on you. You know what they tell you: *Better your 10K time with increased training mileage. Go faster through interval training. Stretch to*

Great Excuses

Admit it. Sometimes, you just want to loaf. If you're so driven to perfection that you need a legitimate-sounding, quasi-rational reason to not go jogging outside in the sleet, here are some good ones:

- *My hair will be a mess.*
- *I just ate.*
- *My mom/wife is afraid this weather will give me pneumonia.*
- *I might miss a phone call.*
- *My muscles don't work in the cold.*
- *My muscles don't work in the heat.*
- *I have a headache.*
- *I wore out my orthotics.*
- *The neighbors might have bought a vicious new dog.*
- *I'm afraid of snakes/cars.*
- *My running shoes are in the laundry.*
- *My only clean running outfit doesn't match my shoes.*
- *I ran last month.*
- *My running partner is sick, and I don't want to be in superior shape when he gets better.*
- *The kiddie stroller has a bum wheel.*
- *My shoelaces are broken.*

increase your stride length and lower your quarter-mile times. Buy these shoes so you can run faster. Faster. Harder.

As long as competitive athletes are our principal role models, we'll be giving people overly heavy advice like that.

The situation isn't necessarily better if you're a noncompetitive beginner: *My doctor says I have to do this. My spouse will find me more attractive if I deny myself comfort and run these miles. I have to lose 25 pounds, which means running 800 miles. This hurts, and my friends all say it will keep hurting.*

This adds up to a lot of pressure and unpleasant associations—probably enough to ruin the sport for most people.

May I recommend some more positive, less destructive thoughts to run through your head? *Running is fun, and it feels good for its own sake. When you breathe deeply, even the air tastes good. I'm not going to let this hurt, I'm taking it easy and staying within my comfort zone. After all these years, I'm getting to see my neighborhood. There's a pretty home I never noticed all the times I drove by this corner. I'm running slowly today, but by next week I'll feel more rested, and I'll be able to run faster. When I get back home, I'll get to watch the news while I do my 10 minutes of stretching. I actually find this relaxing. If running continues to feel better, I always have the option of training seriously and setting up racing goals for myself. But right now, I'm just making sure I enjoy it.*

What? How can *I,* who owe so much to serious competitive running, advocate such laid-back, noncompetitive attitudes?

Because that's what works, even for competitive runners. In my experience, the most consistently successful competitive runners are deliberately low-key about running, most of the time. A 2:12 marathoner of my acquaintance frequently joins women in their fifties for a slow morning run.

The most consistently fast marathon runner in the United States, Doug Kurtis, swears by training at speeds far below his marathon ability: he generally runs seven-minute miles in training, but he's run 60 marathons faster than 2:20 (5:20 per mile), and his best is 2:13:34 (5:06 per mile). So Doug's example shows: even if you want to be extra fit and go fast, you don't get there by hammering yourself every time you go running. Lots of easy workouts tune the body for the occasional race or speed workout.

If you have an ambitious goal, don't let it loom over you. Take it on voluntarily, and let go of it if it's dragging you down. Concentrate on relaxation and enjoyment first; after that, let the goals seem natural and inevitable.

Even runners on competitive teams usually aren't slaves to daily goals. For example, during my college years, I spent about five months per year racing quite seriously on the cross-country and track teams. The other seven months were more relaxed. In winter, our team ran indoor track, but we deliberately

Stretching and Muscle Balance

Your muscles come in opposed pairs. On your upper leg, the quads are opposed by the hamstring. On your lower leg, your shin muscle is opposed by the calf muscles. These opposing pairs have to balance each other. Each muscle is susceptible to problems if its partner is disproportionately stronger and tighter.

For runners, the most common muscle imbalance problem is shin splints. The calf muscles get lots of exercise, particularly in faster runners. All the shin muscle ever gets to do, though, is lift the toes. So the calf muscles get stronger and tighter, while the shin muscle stays weak. The resulting imbalance is the cause of shin splints.

There are other imbalances to watch for. Bike riders who puff up their quad muscles (as all bike riders do) may get problems from a quad-hamstring imbalance.

If you have an imbalance problem, go see a sports-oriented physical therapist or an athletic trainer. They can measure the flexibility and strength of each muscle and tell you if they're in the proper proportions to each other. If they're not, your physical therapist or trainer can prescribe strengthening and/or stretching exercises that will correct the imbalance.

made it low-key, so we wouldn't be putting too much pressure on ourselves. In summer, we'd run a few times per week to maintain fitness but without a racing schedule or other immediate goal. Our chief concern was to show up on campus in September in good enough shape to limp through high-mileage preseason workouts in the wilting mid-Atlantic heat.

These seasons of low-key, unpressurized running are vital to the competitive athlete. We'd approach each competitive season feeling refreshed and ready to dig in. Because we were refreshed, we didn't see the commitment of racing as undue pressure; rather, it was an opportunity we'd looked forward to. And, more than we appreciated at the time, we were glad to relax a bit at the season's end.

Of course, there will always be runners who don't understand that they need physical or mental rest. I've known many runners who would triumphantly arrive each fall after having logged 1,000 miles during the summer. Except for the few with magic, Olympic-caliber bodies, this is a prescription for disaster. Overtrained and overstressed, these runners would peak in the first few weeks of the season, start to deteriorate in October, and find themselves injured and sidelined by the time of the important races in November.

When you do have specific goals, don't take them so seriously. I remember one runner, years ago, who had a goal very important to him: to finish in the top ten in the Philadelphia Marathon. The top ten got

Should You Breathe Hard?

When I was a lad in the Boy Scouts, the Boy Scout Handbook *offered some utterly useless advice: when you go hiking, don't walk so fast that you're out of breath. You should always be able to talk as you hike.*

Yeah, right. Take a 90-pound kid (me), saddle him with a 900-pound backpack (or so it seemed), and tell him to keep up with all the big strong kids. Under these conditions, breath is precious stuff not to be wasted on mere conversation.

Today, when I go running with a friend, we'll frequently talk. And that is how it should be.

So the old Boy Scout Handbook *was correct after all, although it failed to point out that if you're basically sedentary (as I was), even the moderate effort level of hiking will get you out of breath. Hike anyway. As you get more fit, you'll get less out of breath. Don't take that as a sign to go faster and stay out of breath. Instead, take it easy.*

As a runner, you'll develop the ability to run a moderate pace and converse. If you're not there yet, look forward to it.

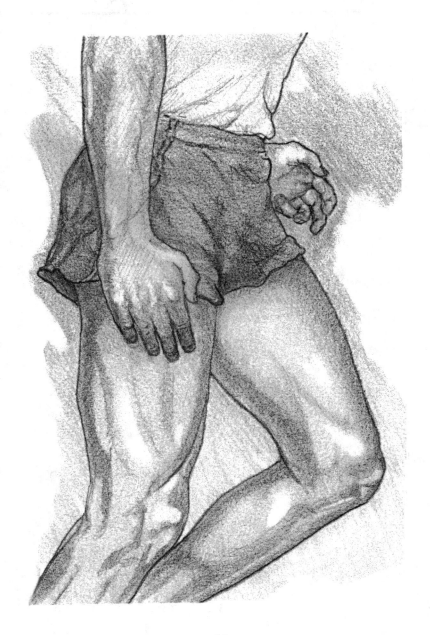

Timex wristwatches for prizes. My friend finished 11th, missing a wristwatch by about 30 seconds. Was he happy to have run a 2:33 marathon? No, he was mad at himself for missing out on an eight-dollar wristwatch. He was visibly angry.

Me, I'd be thrilled to run 2:33. I'd be so thrilled I'd go buy myself a wristwatch to celebrate.

So, what were those folks in Central Park doing wrong? The answer is fairly simple: they weren't allowing themselves to relax. Their mental stress carried over into physical stress. Physical discomfort inevitably followed. As long as running was stressful and uncomfortable for those people, they'd never enjoy it.

Start with the clenched fists. When you clench your fist, you tense most of the muscles in your arm. So immediately your entire arm carriage is tensed up. The problem flows downstream to your shoulders and back. For these unfortunate people, running makes all these muscles tense up. It's enough to make your chiropractor wealthy!

By contrast, a good rule of thumb for running (or for almost any exercise) is this: contract as few muscles as possible. Hold your hands in a loose, half-closed configuration. Let your arms swing naturally. Don't hold them up near your chest; let them fall a bit lower, where they want to go naturally. Occasionally lift your head up, the better to loosen your neck muscles. Every few minutes ask yourself, "What can I do to relax more?" As you mentally check over your body from head to toes, you'll probably discover a muscle you're contracting unnecessarily. Let it flop. You'll be rewarded by less tension, and you may even find you can run faster and easier.

Remember that the best competitive runners—and the happiest exercise-for-health runners—do most of their training at a pace they find easy and non-stressful. And they do relax while they run.

This notion—that running should be graceful and comfortable—is one that came to me only after I spent years doing it the wrong way. My arm motion was strained and artificially tight, my shoulders traced a sine wave through the air, and my whole upper body wiggled with an exaggerated show of unnecessary and uncomfortable motion. Naturally, my face usually showed great strain. I thought all that pain was just part of it. I looked so bad that coaches from opposing schools used to try to help me improve my form. They were motivated, I suspect, in part by the embarrassment of having a runner who looked so dreadful beat their own athletes.

My college coach, Joe Stefanowicz, couldn't keep from rolling his eyes when he watched my form. Can't say as I blame him. He openly despaired of doing anything about it, but he's the one who cured it. The cure: mileage and speed. I was training so long and (on speedwork days) so fast, that I needed a more efficient body motion. Gradually, my improved form just evolved out of necessity.

Today when I run, my arms sway gently by my side, with mostly back-and-forth motion and a minimum of side-to-side motion. My torso is almost

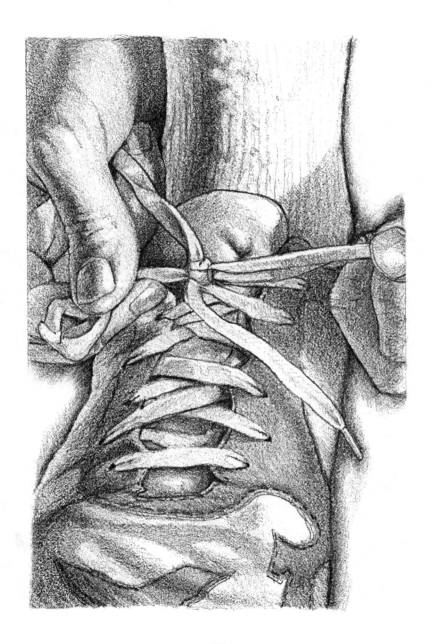

still, bobbing up and down only slightly with each stride. My head is quite still. Every few minutes, I'll mentally check through all my muscles: any face muscles tense? Relax them. Hands? Neck? Any wasted arm motion? Usually I'll find a tense muscle and relax it. The reward: I speed up a little, without any increased effort.

I've used this relaxation technique to go faster in very competitive races. I use it to make eight-minute miles in the summer heat more comfortable. I recommend it to every other runner—most especially the folks who are making themselves hurt in pursuit of good health.

On November 15, 1977, Jim Fixx, author of the best-selling *The Complete Book of Running,* was waiting to appear on a Denver TV talk show. He described the moment:

An old family friend, Patty Hodgins, has come to the studio; afterward she and I plan to have dinner at the Brown Palace.

"Are you getting tired of these interviews?" Patty asks me. I have, as she knows, been at it for three full weeks.

"They're not usually too tedious," I tell her. "I try to treat each one as if it were the first interview I've ever done. It's only when I have to answer a really familiar question that it gets tiresome."

"What's the most familiar question you

hear?" Patty asks me.

I tell her, "I guess it's 'If I've never run before, what would you recommend that I do to get started'."

The interview begins. The show's host, Beverly Martinez, smiles winningly, introduces me, displays the jacket of my book and asks, "Jim, suppose a person has never run before. How should he or she get started?" [1]

Fixx's story pokes fun at an important problem. A novice may feel reluctant to ask the experts. Don't be shy. Novice runners have more links to experienced runners than they may realize. Many experienced runners have had long hiatuses in their running careers: Dr. George Sheehan's hiatus between his college running and his adult running lasted for decades. Many of my old running buddies have let a few years go by here and there and then resumed their manic racing ability. I've never let years go by, but all too often I've let a few months slip.

When we let this much time slide, our bodies become running novices again.

Psychologically, we have an advantage over the "lifelong" novice, but the muscles and lungs don't know that. Our advantage is that we know what to expect when starting up again. We know sore muscles only last a few days and that wheezy feeling is gone in two weeks. We know that discomforts don't last

[1] Fixx, James F., *Jackpot!* (NY, Random House, 1982); p. 67.

Being Prepared

Years ago I was an instructor in an Outward Bound program run by a Detroit-area prep school. The school's students were taken to North Carolina's Smoky Mountains in snowy, rainy March. We hiked our buns off each day, camped out in crude plastic tarps, and ate the canned mackerel and other goodies stuffed into our backpacks. (Hey, when you're that hungry canned mackerel almost starts to taste good.)

To me, the scary thing was how uneven the students' preparation was. Some were physically fit and had equipment for hiking and camping in wet snow. Others had slumber-party sleeping bags and shopping-mall clothing. And some just weren't ready. One kid in particular was smaller than his backpack. The first day, he stumbled on a rock, fell, and injured his knee. He had to leave the group and go back home.

A month-long program of hiking and jogging at home would have prepared him, made him stronger, and enabled him to stay upright and/or probably avoid injury if he did fall.

forever, and we know that we can minimize them simply by relaxing.

All this is a way of saying: Despite the fact that I may have a quarter century of running behind me, I have empathy, many times over for the problems you're encountering while just starting out.

Any sedentary adult starting an exercise program should get a doctor's physical. This is more than just a disclaimer. A decent physical will set your mind at ease, and it may find things you should do something about.

Then I recommend you go for a bunch of walks.

Go for three or four walks per week for at least two weeks. Start with no more than one mile. Increase the distance *gradually.* Every other time you walk, add no more than one half mile to your distance. Keep this up until you feel comfortable at a distance of three miles. Extend the two-week period as necessary to reach your three-miles-with-comfort goal.

Babies *have* to walk before they can run, and it's good policy for everyone else. Walking puts your body on notice: more activity is coming to challenge joints and muscles. You strengthen your ankles so they won't sprain as readily; you warm up those knees; you get blood flowing through little-used veins and capillaries. Your heart and lungs get a gentle workout. Your body can get acclimated to the stresses of moving on your feet—a lost sensation in our post-caveman life-style. You'll be prepared.

Then one day, put on your shoes and go running

A Novice's Weekly Schedule

You're just starting to run. What should your week's schedule look like? No one schedule is perfect, but here's a plausible one:

Sunday: 3 miles on flat ground. Easy pace.

Monday: Rest. Stretch and massage.

Tuesday: 3-mile walk.

Wednesday: 2 miles.

Thursday: Rest.

Friday: 2 miles.

Saturday: Rest.

This schedule gives you 7 running miles, 3 walking miles, and 3 rest days. It uses the walking to help you recover from your running.

Seven miles per week will make you fit and happy, without taking too much time or energy.

instead of walking.

A mile is plenty. Slow is fine. You want this to be a positive experience not a reach for futile goals. Maybe you want to do what I did the very first day I went running back in 1967: run a half mile, walk a quarter mile to rest and recover, then run a half mile.

Don't even try to do your best. There's lots of time for that later. When you're starting out, the thing that will make your body happiest is staying within its limits. Hammer hard and you're sure to find the most injury-prone and most painful parts of your body. The point of hammering is to go fast, and you can't go fast when you're starting out. So don't hammer.

Bring a friend for moral support. Chat about old times.

Become a connoisseur of the things that make loping along enjoyable. Relax, and try to feel fluid. Enjoy the scenery. Don't artificially constrain your stride or arm motion; do what feels natural, while avoiding excess gestures of agony.

Never run two days in a row when you're starting out. It bears repeating: running tears your body down; it's the rest days that replenish it.

Stretch. Massage yourself. If you do manage to mess up and injure yourself, put ice on the injury. (See the separate section on these valuable activities.)

So how much should you run? Here's my call: start with one mile every other day. That's all of four miles per week. *If* you're comfortable with that, you can abruptly increase it to two per day, or eight per

A Gentleman Jogger's
Weekly Schedule

You're not a novice anymore. You've babied your body for a couple months now, and feel more ambitious for a higher weekly mileage. Here's what your week's schedule might look like now.

Sunday: 5 miles. Go hard during fourth mile, with ample warm-up and warm-down.

Monday: Rest. Stretch and massage.

Tuesday: 3 miles.

Wednesday: Rest.

Thursday: 4 miles.

Friday: Rest.

Saturday: 4 miles.

These 16 miles per week will put you in good stead. This is as much as you need to run if you're interested only in fitness. Running more than 16 miles per week is purely for fun.

week. But once you hit double digits, heed the following rule of thumb: your maximum increase in weekly mileage should be five miles every other week. So after a month, your ceiling is 20 miles per week. After three months, this rule of thumb would put your ceiling at 40 miles per week. But by then, most people will reach a point where they don't want to increase their mileage as much as this rule would theoretically allow. Besides, the rule bends to all other contingencies: injuries, illnesses, and your own intuition, which tells you to slack off a bit and let your body catch up with your ambitions.

And finally, especially if you think of this as a spartan activity, associate it with as many pleasurable experiences as possible. For me, this means running on a beautiful trail through the woods, followed by a bottle of Lord Chesterfield ale and a soak in the Jacuzzi. Choose your pleasure.

Sometimes, running falls far short of victory and personal triumphs.

Here's a true story: not long ago, I set out to run three slow miles on a summer day, felt exhausted, and wound up walking home. The heat took its toll, I was out of shape, and my biorhythms were obviously in the trough. But however valid these reasons, I experienced deep discouragement. There wasn't even an injury to blame: I just didn't have the suds. I sure didn't feel like the "most inspirational athlete" that day.

Most sports have setbacks, and running has its fair share. As much as I love this sport, I'm not going to tell you it's perfect or problem-free. The flu may linger for a month. Your job may require a lengthy stay in a hotel on an industrial highway where there's truly no decent place and no scheduled time in your day to run. For all the books and articles on injuries, you may find yours doesn't fit any known mold, and the medical folks you consult are puzzled. All these setbacks, and more, have happened to me.

And running isn't something you do twice a month—that is, not if you want to feel good doing it. Only regular runners enjoy what they're doing. So once you slide down, you have to climb back up.

Some runners avoid those problems by never taking time off. They're the ones with the magic bodies, the ones who never get sick or injured, the ones who never even want a day off, the ones who claim they like shoving out of bed at 5 A.M.

The rest of us have to overcome setbacks. To cope with the disappointment, it helps to remember a few things:

• You're doing this for fun.
• The problems *will* get solved, even if it takes a while.
• You have a whole lifetime to enjoy running, so no matter what event you miss because of an injury, some future fun event will replace it.
• Other activities are fun, too. Enjoy them on their own merits while time and therapy take care of your running problems.

Training Diary

On April 8, 1969, I decided I wanted to start keeping a training diary.

That day, I ran seven 660-yard intervals, averaging 1:53 per interval. The following day I ran six 440s, averaging 69, and I practiced baton passes for the next day's mile relay race.

The log continues through today, when I ran three and a half easy miles through the woods with my dog Frostbite in tow. In between are school records, injuries that dashed my dreams, triumphant wins, disappointing losses, breakups with girlfriends, and ample evidence why I was seriously undertrained for my first marathon.

Start a training diary today. You can go buy a fancy one from a training diary publisher or grab an old calendar they give you at the bank every winter; it doesn't matter. Write down what you did, how it felt, whether you're sore, and the status of any injuries. Total your weekly, monthly, and annual mileage; these figures will give you valuable at-a-glance information. Any other things you add will be your personal imprint.

When a setback does impose, think ahead to make your comeback as good as possible. *Good* means different things to different people. To a runner in the midst of a serious competitive season, it means fast—to get back into racing right away. To a recreational or lifetime sport runner, it might mean slow, measured, and deliberate—trading recovery time for less risk of relapse.

Serious athletes often have trouble understanding that there are big advantages to coming back slowly. For one thing, you avoid the mental stress of trying to recover quickly. The athlete in training gets up every morning wondering if his pulled muscle has healed enough to allow a return to interval training. The weekend 10K runner typically has plenty of other worries; better to write off the next few weeks of running and explore the fun of hiking and cycling than to get Type-A fretful about running.

If you do want to come back quickly from a significant injury, you need close supervision from a coach and/or athletic trainer. You need their expertise to minimize the risk of reinjuring yourself.

I've missed some damn important races, including a Boston Marathon and an NCAA national championship, due to injuries. Over time, I've learned not to fret unduly about these losses. Instead, I focus on a sensible, safe recovery and long-term rehabilitation.

Now let's get back to that hot summer day. A few weeks later, after grimly bootstrapping myself to the point where I could manage a slow jog, I added a

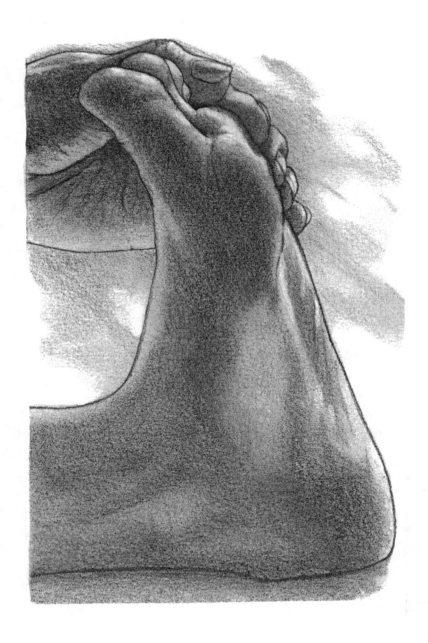

Cross-Training:
Point/Counterpoint

Point: *Cross-training is great. You exercise all the muscles that running ignores. You lessen the pounding on your knees and feet, arguably the most injury-prone body parts. You get the mental refreshment of trying other sports, and you have more ways to have fun. You stay in touch with your running fitness base, while enjoying less austere sports, too. You'll probably have fewer injuries.*

Counterpoint: *Oh, you idealistic fool. Good luck scheduling enough time to be even moderately proficient in all the activities the cross-training proponents want you to sample. Sure, the professional triathletes do it, but when they're done exercising each day, it's time to drop into bed. And the average middle-of-the-pack triathletes? All* they're *good at is buying fancy equipment! They slog through the water, ride bikes with plenty of power but no bike handling, and then jog a bunch of eight-minute miles. What a return on 20 hours of training time per week! If you have only 10 hours to spare, you can be even lousier at three sports, or you can be a darn good runner. Personally, I like being good.*

new discouragement: I pulled a muscle. How? On one of my slow jogs, I tried to go too fast. A few weeks later, again trying to do too much too soon, I reinjured the muscle. Truly, I had maximized the setback and delayed the comeback.

Finally, I decided to take my own advice and recondition myself gradually. Instead of vainly hoping the muscle would abruptly heal and allow me to run the following day, I started going for walks. The walks included steep hills, which provided more-than-adequate cardiovascular challenge, and didn't seem to hurt that muscle. I also rode my stationary bike some for alternate exercise on foggy evenings. I stretched almost as often as I'm supposed to.

I deliberately took it easy on some workouts, interspersed some bicycling with running so as not to tax my aging body with my overeager mind, and commanded myself not to worry just because I was going so slow.

The happy result: I was able to add mileage gradually, my speed improved dramatically, and I built a good foundation for recovery. The entire episode took about five months. Had I been more patient with myself, it would have taken less than half that long. All I would have needed to do was mix walking days with running days before the injuries forced me to, and slow down on my running days. Voilà! Gradual recovery, no injuries.

Whether you're a young, serious runner or an elderly duffer, follow this cardinal rule: when recovering from injuries, don't dare try to do your best. Hold back! Haste makes waste.

If slow runs or alternate-exercise hikes discourage you, think twice—they're the best thing for you. If you were fit and fast before the injury, conservative rehab will preserve much of your fitness base and allow you to return to your previous peak shortly after it's prudent to resume hard training. There's no percentage in rushing your recovery.

There *is* life after injuries.

Sometimes the best thing a runner can do is walk.

Walking is an extremely important part of a runner's overall exercise program. Of course, it's a great way for a nonrunner to ease his or her body into running without undue stress. But it's also a great way for an experienced runner to get a viable aerobic workout at a moment when running wouldn't be such a hot idea.

Maybe you don't have time to dress out, run, shower, and dress back. Maybe you're in a slump, and if you run, you'll run slowly and feel discouraged. Maybe you have a tight muscle susceptible to injury if you run on it. Maybe you just want a change. Maybe you want to take a nonrunning friend out for some exercise, in which case walking can be your common ground.

Maybe you start out on a run, and midway through the day's workout you realize that it's just not your day.

When I polled my old teammates in preparation

Don't Stop Reading Here

Most runners get injuries now and again. Without proper treatment, an injury can stay with you for life. Two books about diagnosing and treating injuries which have long impressed me are:

The Sportsmedicine Book *by Gabe Mirkin, M.D., and Marshall Hoffman (Little, Brown & Co., Boston, 1978). I was astonished by this book. It contained so many of the pearls of wisdom that I thought were known only to my trainer. There was pronation spelled out, demystified, and reduced to plain English. There were shin splints, made preventable. Every other imaginable problem was spelled out. Read this book as a preventive measure, before you get injured.*

Save Your Knees *by James M. Fox, M.D., and Rick McGuire (Dell, New York, 1988). Fox sets out to demystify his profession, and he succeeds admirably. He gives easy-to-understand descriptions of knee injuries, straight talk about prognosis for recovery, and a delightful list of questions with which to shake down your next orthopedic surgeon. You'll learn lots about preventive maintenance and rehabilitation, and there are blunt observations aplenty.*

for this book, several were quite adamant about the importance of walking. (And remember, this comes from runners who are competitive and successful.)

"Learn how to use walking or jogging as part of a run—whether as a rest period in interval work or as a way of extending your distance on the roads," comments Tom Crochunis. "Coaches used to teach young runners to think of walking as a failure to continue running. But easing off can be a good way to break yourself out of a strained workout for a few moments so that you can begin again mentally fresh."

John Devlin uses walking as part of his weekly workout plan. If he can spare an hour or less from his schedule, he goes walking instead of running. That way, he spends zero time in the shower and the entire hour exercising. "If I have half an hour, I can do thirty minutes of walking. But it takes over an hour to do thirty minutes of running." Does this sound like the modest program of someone who doesn't aspire to get very fit? Well, Devlin allocates only six hours per week to exercise—including showering, dressing, and so on—and in the months I was working on this book, he ran a 4:56 mile, a 10:14 two-mile, and a 17:10 5K. Walking must be worth something.

Indeed, a brisk walk pushes your pulse up much like an easygoing jog does. That's the sure measure that it's legitimate exercise.

And if you're having trouble relaxing when you run, maybe you can relax while you walk. Relaxing *has* to be a part of exercise.

I have a list of five miracle cures to prevent injury, or at least minimize it and speed recovery: stretching, massage, warming up, warming down, and ice therapy.

The most important precaution against injury is to stretch several times every day. This advice marks me as a bit of a hypocrite, since I loathe stretching. I do stretch, but I have naturally tight muscles, so stretching is an uphill battle. I preach its benefits with all the personal enthusiasm I muster when I tell my kids to eat their brussels sprouts.

Still, the facts are clear. Limber muscles are far less susceptible to injury than tight muscles. Muscle injuries aren't the only problems stretching can avoid; problems such as knee pain and shin splints can be caused by tight muscles. And stretching is doubly necessary if you want to run fast, because fast running demands a much greater range of motion from your muscles than eight-minute-mile running.

Almost as beneficial as stretching, and a lot more fun, is massage. Massage helps your muscles to clear away metabolic waste products, accelerating the recovery process and reducing soreness to a degree that will astonish you. Massage will even help you sleep better. And you can do it yourself in five minutes per day.

Warming up helps do what stretching was supposed to: it makes you more limber. It gets your system ready for the more demanding part of the workout that you're about to impose on your body.

A warm-down helps you relax, adds more gentle stretching, and does its own part to rid your muscles of metabolic slag.

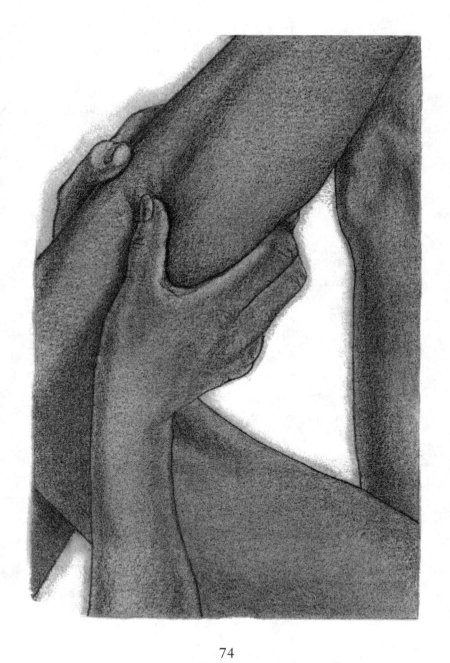

74

And ice, when you've managed to injure yourself, will limit the trauma caused by most injuries and speed your recovery.

Let's start with massage, since that's the fun part.

Many runners don't know about massage. I learned about its benefits through bike racing and gladly imported it to my running.

Massage makes a dramatic difference in how sore you get from a hard workout, and how well you recover. It can make the difference between feeling draggy and feeling spry the following day.

You should massage your own legs after a workout, especially if the workout has been a strenuous one and you suspect your muscles will be feeling sore. After your warm-down and shower or bath, lie on your back with your butt next to a wall and your legs extended upward, heels resting on the wall. (A shag rug is a luxurious touch, if you have one.) Bend one knee toward your chest and massage the calf. Always work toward the heart, kneading the muscle and shaking it occasionally for variety. Switch legs and repeat. Now straighten both legs and do each thigh.

I repeat, the benefits of massage are far more dramatic than you'd guess from reading about it. Those five minutes will hasten your recovery by at least a day.

Warming up and warming down together take 15 minutes, but they give back weeks of injury avoidance. Warming up means an ample period of slow running—a bare minimum of five minutes' worth—before feeling your oats for the day. Serious competitive athletes often warm up for two or three miles (just as I used to do when I was fast). The point of the warm-up is to run at a speed too slow to possibly cause any injury. While you do that, your muscles, lungs, and heart all have time to wake up. Your blood circulation and breathing are gradually brought up to speed, and the muscles are warmed up and made as limber as they are going to get that day. You can vividly see the importance of warming up if you ever race without doing so. Race pace is a shock to your system, and it will simply feel wrong if you aren't warmed up first.

After you're done running, spend five to ten minutes in a brisk walk or slow jog. Your heart rate will stay elevated, so you'll have good blood circulation through your muscles. The elevated blood circulation helps to carry slag out of the muscles and into the bloodstream, where it can be cleaned away by the appropriate organs (such as the kidneys).

A warm-down, I've noticed in semicontrolled experiments, can make a big difference in how sore you get from a hard workout, how well you recover, and how well you can run the following day.

And the best thing about your warm-down is that it leads to your massage.

I do hope you learn a better attitude toward stretching than I have. I'd be a much faster runner today, and I would have avoided many pulled muscles over my life, if I had never slacked off on my

Pronation and You

Flat feet—low arches—are largely a symptom of the real problem: excess pronation. Pronation is rotation of your foot inward. If you wear out the inside edges of your shoes, you're probably an overpronator. The problem is that the rotation of the foot is transferred through the ankle up to the knee, where by causing "runner's knee" it causes the kneecap (patella) to rub uncomfortably against other surfaces.

Podiatrists, certified athletic trainers, physical therapists, and orthopedic surgeons can often help, usually by prescribing knee-stabilizing exercises, arch supports, orthotics (they're custom-molded arch supports), and, yes, stretching.

There was a time when no one knew how to solve pronation-induced knee problems. Now, the knowledge is widespread among sports-savvy medical professionals. Seek out care from someone who knows his or her stuff, study the problem, be patient with your recovery, and you may find yourself fully recovered someday.

stretching. Stretching makes you limber, and being limber is one of the prerequisites to running that four-minute mile you've dreamed about. For that matter, being limber sure helps you run a six-minute mile. And a seven-minute mile.

The most important thing about stretching is to do it consistently. That means often. Easy, gentle stretching for five minutes twice a day, or even three times a day, will benefit you more than a long session once per day. Stretch when you're waiting for a train, listening to the news, or waiting for a pot of water to boil. Stretch when you're sick and can't run; it's a way for you to work on your fitness without exercising per se, and you'll have the new advantage of being more limber when you get back to running.

Never do any stretch to the point of discomfort. Stretch only to the point where your muscles are tight, and not beyond. Each stretch should be for a duration of one to two minutes. If you do this often enough, your muscles will gradually become more limber. But it does take weeks. Persistence is essential.

If I've ever had a stretching success story, it's been my use of a slant board for calf stretching. I stand on the slant board, toes elevated above my heels, whenever I'm going to be standing in one spot anyway. I keep it in the kitchen to use while I'm washing dishes, talking on the telephone, etc.

You can make a slant board in 10 minutes with a circular saw; it's time well spent, and a good excuse to go buy the saw if you don't already own one. To make a slant board, get a scrap of 5/8-inch plywood big enough to stand on (mine is 14" x 14") and two scraps of 2 x 4s, each 14 inches long. Cut the 2 x 4s into wedge-shaped pieces. Make the wedges 20 degrees if you are naturally limber. My wedges are 15 degrees, which is fine for me. Nail or screw the wedges to the bottom of your plywood sheet. Now set it on the floor, wedges facing down, and you have your slant board to stand on.

If you incorporate your slant board into your daily routine, it will give you a good 10 minutes per day of gentle calf stretching, without taking any time of its own.

Stretching produces better results more quickly if you use the contract-relax method. You put yourself in the stretched position, then holding that position, contract the muscle you're trying to stretch. In other words, you try to push the limb against the wall/table/floor, which is constraining it. After about 10 seconds of contraction, relax the muscle. Now you'll find it's more limber, and you can stretch it a bit more without discomfort. Repeat this once.

There are dozens of possible stretches, but I'm going to tell you about the four basic ones.

• Hamstring stretch. Stand beside a table, put one foot up on the table. Hold your hips still, bend over, and try to touch your toes. This exercise is a natural for the contract-relax method. Just try to push the table through the floor by exerting downward pressure with your heel.

• Quad stretch. Lie on your stomach and bend one knee, bringing your foot to your rear end (and

The True Oppressors of Women

. . . are the cretins who make high-heeled shoes fashionable.

Wear high heels regularly and watch yourself become such an orthopedic cripple that running becomes all but impossible.

The heel lift in an average running shoe is about one centimeter. A high heel has—what? Two inches? Your Achilles tendon atrophies and shrinks when it's kept bunched up by high heels. Then if you put on running shoes and try to run, the repeated exercise will combine with the unfamiliar (to your calf muscles) range of motion to promote injury.

If you must wear high heels regularly, spend at least 10 minutes per day standing on your slant board, stretching your calves. And write to your congressman/woman and get him or her to sponsor National Flat Heel Week. The only person who deserves high-heeled shoes is Imelda Marcos.

don't let your rear end rise up while you do this).
Reach behind you and grasp your ankle. If this
doesn't stretch your quad significantly, raise the thigh
off the floor. If your quads are so tight you can't reach
your ankle in the first place, grab a towel wrapped
around the ankle.

• Groin stretch. Sit on the floor and bring the soles
of your feet together in front of you. Try to lower
your knees to the floor. Use the contract–relax
method by holding your knees down with your
elbows, and pushing up against the elbows. When
you relax, apply a steady pressure downward against
your knees, and be sure not to bounce.

• Wall stretch. Stand two feet away from a wall,
put your hands flat on the wall, and lean into the wall.
This stretches your calves. You can add a simultaneous
stretch to the pectoral muscles in your chest by doing
this exercise facing a corner instead of a flat wall.

There are countless other stretching exercises you
can do; generally, they're different ways of stretching
the same muscles addressed above. What's important
is that you do them regularly. Take it from one who
knows: once you let your muscles get tight, it takes a
long time to get them limber again.

Sometimes, you mess up. You step in a pothole
and twist an ankle. You go too fast on a sore muscle
and pull it.

Thank God for ice, which will minimize the down
time these injuries cause you.

Left to its own devices, your body does something

dumb when you get an injury. It bleeds into the wounded area. The more bleeding you get, the longer the time to heal. Ice causes the blood vessels to constrict. Voilà! Bleeding is minimized. Swelling is minimized.

Get a big bag of crushed ice and set it on a thin towel on the injured area, as soon as possible after the injury. (Each minute's delay means more swelling and bleeding.) Leave the ice there for 20 minutes. Ice the injury each day for three days. And then, particularly if it's a joint injury, get proper medical attention. After the initial three-day icing period, an athletic trainer or physical therapist can supervise high-tech treatments such as ultrasound and contrast baths (two-minute intervals of ice water and hot water) to speed your recovery.

Ice is really only one part of the well-known four-part approach to injuries: rest, ice, compression and elevation (RICE). If you have any significant injury, you should seek medical attention to guide you in application of these techniques, but it's hard to go wrong starting out with an ice pack.

———————————

[A] runner . . . staggered into the locker room after finishing in the District of Columbia 25-kilometer championships one year. The race had been conducted despite a blinding snowstorm, which made it impossible to see more than five yards ahead. The runner sat on a bench next to Ed O'Connell, a government employee. For

several minutes both competitors were too cold
to talk. Finally the other runner turned to
O'Connell and chattered through half-frozen
lips: "Did you see those crazy people out there
trying to drive in that weather?"[1]

I can relate. The two good marathons I ran both
took place during violent snowstorms. The two
mediocre marathons I ran were during nice spring
weather. Some of my better track performances were
during blistering heat.

With preparation, you can be *comfortable* running in
adverse weather. You can *like* it. When you can
prevail over heat or cold, you'll realize that it's yet
another way that being a runner empowers you.

Yet every time the weather gets hot or cold,
especially hot, you'll see jillions of doctors appearing
on local TV newscasts urging people not to exercise
outdoors for fear of dire consequences.

Yes, the consequences can be deadly. So for John
Q. Jogger, "don't exercise" is the only safe advice.
But a sophisticated athlete who knows his own
limitations, and also knows why and how adverse
weather stresses the body, can expand the performance
envelope a bit wider.

Heat is the more ominous and complicated threat,
so we'll consider that first.

[1]Higdon, Hal, *On the Run from Dogs and People*
(The Chicago Review Press, 1979); p. 59.

Potassium and Your Conscience

Sweating lots? Need to replenish your body electrolytes? Need potassium but hate bananas?

Boy, do I have good news for you.

Chocolate is high in potassium! (So are raisins and coconuts, but that's not nearly as much fun.)

And you can wash down that chocolate with a hot cup of strong brewed coffee—your favorite high-potassium beverage. Then sit down to some high-potassium beef (not the fat, though; it has almost no potassium). Make sure you fry your vegetables; that way they have more potassium than steamed and/or water-soaked vegetables.

Of course, chocolate and beef are high in fat, but who says life is perfect?

Your muscles generate heat as a waste by-product of generating motion. Every time you move a muscle, about two thirds of the food energy you consume produces waste heat; only one third produces motion. In winter, this waste heat is welcome, but in summer you need to be rid of it.

Your body is continuously generating heat—through muscle motion, through chemical goings-on in your visceral organs—and dissipating it. You dissipate heat through your skin. In cool weather, you can reject heat to the outside air by four mechanisms: radiation, conduction, convection, and evaporation. In warm weather, radiation and conduction don't work, and convection gets less effective as the air temperature increases.

Of course, you already knew that sweating was your body's way of making evaporative cooling occur. But sweating is effective only because the heat generated by the body core is brought to the skin. Your bloodstream performs a function like that of the coolant in your car's radiator, carrying core heat out to the skin surface, where (you hope) evaporative cooling will cool the skin and hence the blood. Your now-cooled blood can return to the body core to pick up more heat and bring it back out to the skin.

This heat transfer function of the bloodstream comes at a cost. For it to occur, the blood vessels near the skin must dilate, allowing greater blood volumes than normal to circulate near the skin.

Thus the heart has to work harder because it's pumping additional blood volume.

This is where many runners put their ass in a sling. Hot or cold, they run "their" pace—let's say, for sake of argument, that it's 7:30 per mile. It's hot out. They aren't breathing any harder than when they run that same pace on a cold day. The pace feels familiar, and on a cold day it might be easy. But the heart is working much harder to maintain adequate blood flow and blood pressure. This is one reason why an "easy" pace may be overdoing it.

On a hot day, you can expect your body core temperature to rise during the course of a workout. This is because your body slowly loses the battle to keep the temperature down to the regulation 98.6°. In an extreme case, a runner on the verge of Deep Trouble may reach a core temperature around 105°, hopefully just at the finish of the run, where a cold wet towel waits to refresh you. (Of course, if you're running ultradistances or if you're exercising by way of another sport, such as bicycling, which keeps you active for hours on end, you dare not let your core temperature rise nearly so much.)

There are several ways to keep yourself safe: You can slow down. (I sure do. Typically, my summer workouts are forty to eighty seconds per mile slower than my winter runs.) You can go a shorter distance, so you have less time to drive up your core temperature. In general, when warm weather arrives, you should dabble in small doses of hot-

weather exercise, so your heart can acclimate to these greater demands. (Walking is a sensibly cautious way to acclimate yourself to hot weather.)

And you can drink. Boy, can you drink.

I've been known to sweat off six pounds of water (that's three quarts) in a 40-minute, six-mile run. (I measured the water loss by weighing myself before and after on a beam-balance scale.) Even in cold weather, I bet I never sweat less than two pounds (one quart) over that distance. What these numbers tell you is important, because you are considered dehydrated after you sweat about two percent of your ideal lean body weight, and my measurements show how easy it is to exceed that tiny percentage. This water loss causes your blood volume and your blood pressure to decrease, creating extra work for your already overburdened heart.

It's an excellent idea to use a scale to monitor your water weight loss. (Beware of cheap home bathroom scales though; they aren't accurate enough for this purpose. Note that cheap digital scales aren't any more accurate than cheap old-fashioned scales.) A good rule would be to put a length limit on your workouts, based on anticipated water weight loss. Measure your weight loss each workout, write it down along with the temperature and distance, and you'll soon know what you can expect. Start out by assigning yourself a three-pound limit. If that doesn't cause you discomfort, slowly increase the limit.

Drinking during a workout is an excellent idea, but it has limitations. Most runners don't want to drink

Clothing and Temperature

Some runners wear too much in warm weather, or too little in cool weather.

People wear too much clothing either because they think one should always wear a running suit to go running or because they want to simulate hot weather in training.

People wear too little clothing because they think they're so tough they don't need any. When I was a young fool, I was often guilty of this sin, venturing out in subfreezing weather with no tights or sweats. Don't make that mistake; cold air can injure your knees.

It's essential to wear a cap in colder weather. Your body has an infinite ability to lose heat through the head. A long run without a cap could beget hypothermia. (I prefer acrylic knit caps on all but the coldest days; wool caps are usually too warm.)

When you cover your hands, gloves may not be the best choice. Many runners like to use old socks. The socks provide the right amount of warmth, while leaving your fingers free to relax inside. I actually prefer old socks with so my hands don't overheat. In a race you can just throw them away if your hands get too warm. Different people have different preferences. Here are mine:

•Above 70°: Headband to divert sweat from eyes; no shirt or a sleeveless shirt ("singlet").

•55° to 70°: Headband optional; T-shirt.

•45° to 55°: Headband essential, this time to hold hair down and provide slight warmth; two T-shirts, one of which is long-sleeved; short tights (reaching to the knees) or thin, sheer tights. Hand warmers. Some runners need a cap at this temperature.

•35° to 45°: Knit cap, three shirts, one of which is long-sleeved, long tights.

•25° to 35°: Add a bandana around the neck and an additional shirt. At this temperature, polypropylene or other miracle fiber is essential; cotton's tendency to get clammy is lethal.

•Below 25°: May add Windbreaker and/or thicker shirts and/or warmer tights.

very large quantities, so you might consume a half-pint of water while you're in the process of sweating five pints. You have to carry water with you, or stop at a drinking fountain. Use water stations in a race, but don't expect to fully rehydrate yourself with a dinky three-ounce cup of water.

If you want to run as much as possible in hot weather, listen to your body and stay within your limits. Let me tell you what it's like to be right on the ragged edge of disaster: I've had summer workouts where I elevated my core temperature so much that when I got back home I didn't dare stop moving. My body was so overheated that it depended on the windchill factor from my moving through the air. If I stopped and sat down, the decrease in windchill factor would mean that warmer blood was returning to my overheated body core. And I'd immediately feel faint. Fortunately, I understood the mechanism well enough to know what to do. I'd get up and jog up and down the driveway until I'd lost a little more body heat. Then I went inside my home and stood in front of a huge fan.

A well-conditioned athlete's sweat is mostly water. Don't worry about losing too much salt (sodium chloride). You don't need to take salt tablets, and if some un-American diet means you aren't getting enough salt, your body will crave it, and you'll find that salting your food is almost an involuntary reflex.

On the other hand, you may run low on

potassium. Potassium deficiency is a leading cause of muscle cramps. Potassium is found in fruits, vegetables, and fruit juice. One traditional favorite source for athletes is the banana.

Unless you're a biochemical expert, don't take potassium pills. Don't use dietary "light salt" either, since it's one-half potassium chloride. Use herbs and garlic instead. Overdoses of potassium can and *do* kill people; avoid that unwanted consequence by getting smaller quantities of potassium through your good diet. (As one doctor friend of mine put it, "If I had my way, potassium pills would be a prescription drug.")

When you watch the doctors on television, they may warn you about "heat exhaustion" without ever explaining what heat exhaustion is. That's typical. The term has been used loosely to refer to a number of related medical conditions. If you look it up in a first-aid book, you may see this ambiguity reflected in hopelessly vague definitions. In general, heat exhaustion is caused by dehydration and/or too much or too little salt. The consequences may differ in individual cases.

One common kind of heat exhaustion is an overall malaise that builds up over a period of days. It's more often caused by loss of water. Sweating and urinating eight pounds of water per day, and only drinking five or six, would be a good way to get this heat exhaustion. If you keep exercising without properly replenishing your fluids, your blood volume drops, and along with it your blood pressure. In an extreme case, you go into shock. Heatstroke may follow unless you're fed fluids and treated for shock.

Heatstroke is a very specific malady. And it is truly deep doo-doo. It occurs when your core temperature gets too high. The high temperature makes the body's thermostat (the hypothalamus, located in the brain) malfunction. The hypothalamus gets so confused that it stops trying to cool the body down. The overheated body actually stops sweating. The core temperature skyrockets as high as 110°, the brain is literally poached, and the victim becomes unconscious and dies.

Signs of approaching heatstroke: your body is overheated and your skin is hot and red. But you may feel a chill, much like when you have the flu. (That chill is a sign of a malfunctioning hypothalamus.) Other signs: deteriorating vision, breathing and thinking, and throbbing pressure in the head.

Treatment for heatstroke: lay the victim's body down, with the feet elevated a foot higher than the head. Apply ice and fluids to the skin quickly to bring the temperature down. When the victim starts to shiver, stop the treatment so you don't reduce the temperature too much. Summon medical aid. *Hurry!*

With those cheery thoughts behind us, let's turn our attention to cold weather. One problem is that of social status. As Ralph St. Clair, a bicycling, running-to-work commuter puts it, "People who used to suspect you were crazy will now be absolutely certain." Sometimes it's hard to convince your spouse or friends that you are comfortable and happy running in your underwear when it's only 10°.

The heat generated by exercising keeps you warm, but your body needs help from clothing, and that's where some help from fiber science comes in handy. Cold weather, particularly cold rainy weather, is an area where today's synthetic miracle fibers reign supreme. Old-fashioned cotton long johns do have their place; they are great when it's 45° to 55° and dry, and you won't be out for more than thirty or forty minutes. But when it's colder, rainy, foggy or you'll be out longer, cotton is rotten. It soaks up your sweat and remains clammy, cooling you off and never drying out itself.

The cheapest of the miracle fibers is polypropylene, and that's what my cold-weather running gear is made from. Polypropylene, by the way, has a nice soft texture, which feels pleasant next to the skin, despite the polysyllabic name. It sucks moisture away from the skin and expels it to the outside air. The fabric itself can't get soaked and clammy. It's ideal for insulation under demanding conditions, such as a cold rain.

Other proprietary fabrics from the various manufacturers offer other attributes: better insulation, waterproof construction, wicking away of moisture, and so on. Consider them seriously; they may be a worthwhile investment for your own foul-weather needs.

Always wear a knit cap if it is cold enough to tolerate wearing one. In freezing temperatures, your body can lose more heat through the head than you can replenish through generating heat. Since hypothermia (loss of body heat) is just as deadly as heatstroke, you don't want to risk it. I keep a collection of several knit caps, with varying degrees of warmth, so I can always have the perfect one for that day's temperature.

Cold-weather running brings added opportunities to injure oneself.

Your muscles are colder, hence tighter, hence more susceptible to injury. If you feel good and run fast on a cold day, you can be rewarded with a pulled hamstring that takes a month or more to heal. The twin remedies: run slower and, if you insist on strenuous running in the cold, warm up a lot before starting the hard part. (Our cross-country team used to begin some of its November workouts with a relaxed four-mile-long warm-up. Only after that warm-up would we begin our hill climbs, repeat half-mile intervals, or other high-effort training.)

Cold weather brings ice and snow. Shoes with an aggressive tread are a mandatory safety precaution; so is careful selection of your route. Still, you'll always run the risk of slipping and falling. Run carefully so you minimize that risk, and plan your moves so the consequences are minimized if you do fall.

Hypothermia is the cold-weather counterpart to rising core temperature in hot weather. If you are inadequately dressed and not producing enough body heat, your core temperature will decrease as you remain outside. Usually, runners aren't outdoors long enough to make this a problem, but you could always be the exception by wearing a cotton sweatshirt and no hat for a 20-mile workout during a cold rain. And if you like other outdoor sports, be they hunting, hiking, camping, boating, canoeing, cycling, or whatever, make sure you have a plan to avoid hypothermia. It's a killer, and it can kill even when the ambient air temperature is relatively mild (55° or so).

Athletes from other sports, notably bicycling, will marvel that your toes don't freeze off. I've never had cold feet running in 0°, but I've had major foot agony bicycling in 40°. From this I conclude that running pumps blood in and out of the feet, keeping them warm. It's a free benefit, so enjoy it.

What is speed? If you run 100 yards in 10 seconds, you're going only 20.5 mph. The four-minute mile, which remains at the pinnacle of human accomplishment, is a mere 15 mph. Heck, my best 100-yard dash time was only a shade better than 16 mph. For most good distance runners, the height of ecstasy is completing a long race, say a 10K, in anything better than 10 mph (6:00 per mile).

We naturally think of miles per hour in an automobile context, and that's why these numbers seem so boringly slow. In a running context, they're fast enough to be fun. At 10 mph, the scenery starts

Mornings or Afternoons?

People who look at running as a spartan act of self-denial are likely to see it as an early-morning activity. At 6:00 A.M., when all decent people are hugging their pillows, the runner is out flogging his unwilling body.

There are good reasons for running in the afternoon instead of the morning. Your body is warmed up and more limber. Your muscles are chemically cleaned out. (Slag tends to pool in them as you sleep.) Most people feel better in the afternoon; I know I do. If you're training to race, you can run faster workouts in the afternoon.

If your schedule forces you to run in the mornings, no harm done; it's still running. But if you want to race, try to do some of your harder, faster runs in the afternoons (like on weekends). This will train your body to go faster.

A final note: some runners go out twice a day. World-class types have the talent to work their bodies that hard, but the rest of us are usually better off with one workout per day. This permits a faster, higher-quality workout.

to blur because the runner is concentrating on the race. And you get to be near the front of the field, with all the fast people.

But most runners never go anywhere near that fast. I submit that there are three reasons why. Two of them can be overcome if you so desire. They are:

• Your genetic heritage. This is the one you can't change. Some people were born to be slow runners. According to one physical therapist I know, some of his patients are born with such inappropriate biomechanics for running that they really should switch to a different sport.

• You've got to become accustomed to the feel of intense competition. Most of today's runners think they're there, but they're not.

• You've got to train for speed. Those nice, bucolic runs through the countryside are the foundation of your training, but the speed comes from intense interval workouts.

Now let's look at the things you *can* overcome in your quest for speed.

Racing hard, really hard, is tough work. Many of the folks running eight- and nine-minute miles think they're working hard. They pant like crazy, their pulses go as fast as a drum roll, they're hungry and thirsty after the race. That's pretty good evidence they're running as fast as they can go, right?

Wrong. All those sensations can accompany a relatively calm jog in the park. Ask any of the faster runners; true do-your-best racing demands a level of emotional intensity and a focusing of mental and physical energy that does not come naturally.

Moreover, running as fast as your body truly can demands an effort level and pace that seem insanely fast. When you're really running at race pace, you are on the verge of collapse. You feel like you can maintain this pace for maybe 100 more yards, but the finish line is still three miles away.

What experience tells you is that if you feel that way and you just keep going, you can keep going for miles feeling that way. You can feel horrible, as if you'll collapse in the next two steps, but you don't collapse—instead, you keep going at that same insane speed.

(Some important caveats here: I'm not talking about marathons, which are so long that they demand an entirely different strategy. Nor am I talking about the first mile of a race, during which any ill-trained fool can run too fast for his own good. Nor am I talking about a recommended strategy for first-time competitors.)

Runners everywhere have learned through experience that they can maintain that speed and that effort level. But if ordinary sane people had to guess whether they could keep going that fast, based only on how they feel at that moment, they'd be certain the answer was no.

So real racing puts you on the brink of disaster. You're running so fast and hard that if you ran the teeniest bit faster, you really would collapse in oxygen debt. How can you tell where that dividing line is?

That knowledge comes from experience.

A Beginning Racer's Weekly Schedule

You're not running just for cardiovascular fitness anymore. You run because you like it and want to go faster. You want to run races up to 10K (6.2 miles) comfortably. Here's a typical week's schedule.

Sunday: 10 miles. Slow and easy, with just a few hard hill climbs and fartlek bursts of energy in the middle of the run.
Monday: Rest. Stretch and massage.
Tuesday: 5 miles easy.
Wednesday: 6 miles. Some fartlek in the middle.
Thursday: 5 miles easy.
Friday: Rest. Stretch and massage.
Saturday: 4 miles easy.

These 30 miles per week will take you about eight or nine hours, including dressing and shower time. They'll give you the mileage base you need to attack the 10K distance with loftier goals than just finishing.

Much of the experience comes from training for speed, which we'll deal with a bit later. You learn what various paces feel like. You learn that you can run fast for a short, measured interval.

Another part of the experience comes from racing itself. Let's use the example of a five-mile race. You take the first mile fairly easy, say, 20 to 30 seconds slower than your all-out mile pace. Now you're warmed up, and into the groove of the race. It's about now that you settle into the speed and the effort level described above. It's important that you wait until the initial flurry of excitement is long gone, because otherwise you'll go anaerobic.

Obviously, this is not a foolproof process. The risk of being a rabbit, of going too fast at the start of a race and then fading badly, is high, and everyone makes that mistake at some point during a racing career. (I've lost some important races that way.) But by listening to your loudly protesting body, you can learn the difference between a hard pace you can barely maintain and an anaerobic pace you can't maintain.

This ragged-edge-of-disaster running is hard for some people to warm up to. Obviously it hurts.

But look beyond the hurt to the rewards if you want to understand this sport's attraction. As you gain racing experience, and use Zen-like concentration to focus your energy, it hurts less and less. When I've been in good shape for racing, I don't think of the race as hurting. I just think of it as being a lot of work, and an awesome example of how well I can focus my energy.

The reward? Wonderment at how fast you go. You get to tell yourself, I did *that?* I ran *how* fast? You get to reminisce about how astonished you were at your own speed. Free. For the rest of your life. It will have a permanent and positive effect on your self-confidence, self-esteem, and knowledge of how deep inside yourself you can dig when there's a task to be done.

Because racing feels so awesome, runners who enter the sport as teenagers usually have a lifelong competitive advantage over runners who start as adults. The reason: 40-year-olds are aware of their own mortality. The way you feel when you're running on the edge of disaster can be damn scary for a middle-aged runner, feeling this way for the first time. The 40-year-old who has been running that way for 25 years knows she or he can get away with it.

Most nominally competitive runners, the ordinary middle-aged folks you see in 10K races, don't know what they could accomplish if they did speed workouts. They're much slower than they could be.

Now, there's nothing wrong with that. Speed is not a virtue in and of itself. But the anecdotal evidence suggests that these folks aren't as fast as they could be. Casual chitchat among runners and many of the letters to *Runner's World* magazine seeking training advice, reveal a common profile. It seems like every 45-minute 10K runner is someone who pounds down 40 miles per week, weighs 130 pounds, and is young enough that age is no excuse. Why

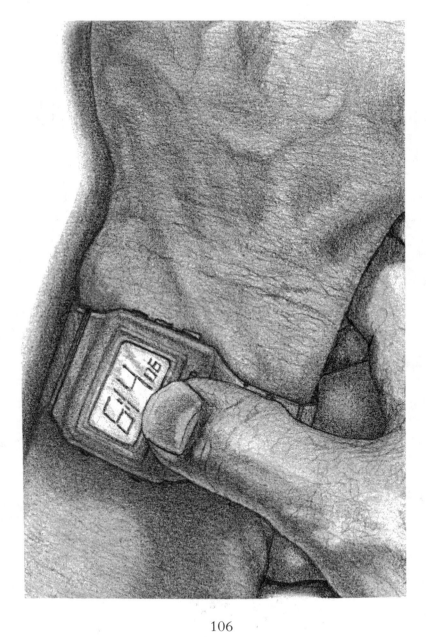

shouldn't someone that lean, and that optimally trained, be running these things in 35 minutes?

Many of them can. All they have to do is change—not increase—their training for about two months. As for this change, it means your mileage will not go up. But instead of running all the miles at a steady pace, you'll do speedwork two or three days per week. The speedwork—timed interval workouts, fartlek (literally, "speed play," varying the pace of a run), and untimed repetitions—will increase your pace and help you adjust mentally to running faster.

Those enjoyable long, steady distance (LSD) workouts will remain the bedrock of your training, but if they're all you do, you'll never go very fast. (Well, almost never; there are a few exceptional people in this big world.) Most folks will find that LSD training brings them to a relatively slow plateau (usually slower than seven minutes per mile).

Speed workouts, when you first do them, hurt. And they make you go fast. As you do them more often, you try to do two things: you try to go faster, and you try to convert the hurt into a simple focusing of your attention and energy. (That's that Zen-like stuff, to teach yourself to increase your effort level in races.)

If you do all this, you'll be transformed as a runner. I promise. When you enter your next race over a familiar distance, your time will plummet. You'll run more smoothly and gracefully. (The demands of speed force you to.)

Biomechanically, you'll be increasing both your leg speed and your stride length. You'll push off more

Accuracy in Measurement

Some runners do all their running on the track, just so they know exactly how far they've run.

There's no way to measure a road course so exactly. A car odometer isn't very accurate, and that 2.3-mile loop around your neighborhood might really be 2.1 miles. But is that really important?

I can tell you all about the scenery on the track: VISITORS/HOME. The broad jump pit. Empty grandstands. The high jump and pole vault pits. A closed and locked hot dog stand.

Now, how about road scenery? Hummingbirds. Friends' houses. Trees. Paths in the woods. And animals. The woods are cooler in summer, sheltered from the wind in winter.

Sure, I have many fond memories of running on the track, but only when the mission is speedwork. The rest of the time, I'll happily accept a 15 percent error in distance measurement so I can enjoy myself.

If you want to know the precise distance of a road course, go to your nearest backpacking store and buy U.S. Geological Survey maps for your area.

with your toes, getting more spring out of each step.

There is a downside: you'll be running much closer to your physical limits, and your risk of injury increases. Listening to your body and heeding common wisdom about prudent training are the important safeguards. (Even so, you'll probably prang yourself with a pulled muscle at some point. In hindsight, you may say, "I noticed that calf was a little sore, but didn't worry about it at the time." Now you know that the little soreness was your warning.)

Doing speedwork alone is theoretically possible, but I've never known anyone who could stand it. It's much, much tougher mentally than sharing the misery with a group of fellow masochists. The difficulty can be measured; whenever I've tried to run timed speedwork alone, my times have been about five to ten seconds per half mile slower than I'd do with a group. And the slower solo runs invariably feel harder. The moral of the story: find some other folks to join you.

Here are several typical speed workouts you might do.

Roadside fartlek: Go on a run of five or six miles. Hold back and run slowly the first two miles so you're warmed up and well rested as you enter the third mile. Now pick a spot about one-eighth mile away. (Telephone poles, road signs, and the crests of hills make great spots.) Run harder, much harder, until you reach that spot, and don't allow yourself to slow down. After you pass that spot, slack off to a slow jog. Two minutes later, pick another spot—this time closer—and maintain an all-out sprint. Jog slowly for two minutes, then run a longer stretch—say, a half mile—at slightly above your normal cruising pace. When you get close to home, resume your normal plod, so your last half mile or so is a nice mellow warm-down.

The essence of fartlek is spontaneity. You vary your pace according to whim. You don't record your performance with a stopwatch. You challenge yourself and embark on strides and sprints before you feel completely recovered from the previous one. You use uphill sprints to vary the challenge. You whimsically pick telephone poles and the speed with which you run toward them.

Timed track intervals: These are the workouts that give you reams of data about your condition. Find a quarter-mile track and a stopwatch. Run about two miles to warm up, stop and stretch gently, run slowly for another half mile to get yourself as limber as possible, and get ready for the workout that hurts. You run a specific distance—say, a half mile—for time, jog a lap slowly to recover, then repeat that distance. You use the stopwatch to record your time, and you try to keep all your intervals that day at a constant speed.

Someone getting started with interval training might run three half miles and call it a day. The third one will hurt enough to make it an easy decision, but with experience you'll learn to endure four. Maybe five.

A distance runner in great condition might do six half miles. Or four one miles. Or ten quarters. My most exotic track workout consisted of a pair of two-mile runs, followed by a one-mile run. In the fading November twilight, we would manage a pair of 10:20s, then knock off that last one mile in about 5:00, wearing heavy training shoes and baggy sweatpants. Ah, to be young again.

Track intervals can be stressful to both the mind and body, so heed these tips to make them less so.

• Don't do distances shorter than one half mile for time unless you have good on-site coaching to monitor your stretching and work load. The reason: the shorter you run, the faster you run, and the faster you run, the more likely you are to give yourself a pulled muscle. For the same reason, never take any shortcuts in your stretching or your warm-up and warm-down.

• Don't race against your training companions. Make it a cooperative effort to run the agreed-upon time. Take turns being the designated leader for the interval. The leader sets the pace, and the other runners fall in behind. Having an assigned leader and an assigned pace will greatly reduce the stress of interval running. If this technique is too communistic for you, maintain your assigned positions until the last quarter mile, then cut loose.

• Don't start the interval like a race. The last thing you need to hear when you're trying to relax in the face of strenuous exercise is "Get set, go!" Instead, start running 10 yards before the start line. Accelerate toward the start line, so you're at training speed as you cross the line. That way, when the stopwatch starts,

A Serious Competitor's
Weekly Schedule

Most of the year you run slow and easily to build your fitness base, but in the week preceding an important race you treat yourself to this hedonistic schedule.

Sunday: 10 miles.
Monday: Slow and easy 4-mile run.
Tuesday: 3 miles warm-up, then two 3-mile time trials on road course, with walking/jogging mile in between, then one mile warm-down. Record your times and do this workout weekly, looking for faster times over the season. (Don't compare these times with anything but other times on the same course.)
Wednesday: 4 miles warm-up, 10 hill climbs (up and down a hill one quarter mile long), then one mile warm-down.
Thursday: 4 miles easy.
Friday: Rest. Stretch and massage.
Saturday: Race. Race distance plus warm-up and warm-down is 8 miles.

This is 47 miles per week. The interval and hill-climb workouts are from my training diary. You can run fast on training like this.

you're already at speed.

• Get a friend to man the stopwatch and shout your times to you. Schools and colleges recruit team managers for this job; if you're not in school anymore, you can impose on a friend, spouse, or child. Having someone to do this is far superior to squinting at your wrist. Thank your manager profusely; it's a dull job.

Untimed intervals: This is a great way to run in a relatively small area, say, around the perimeter of an athletic field, or a short path through a park. A path that's too short for a satisfying distance run (because, well, what distance runner wants to do 10 laps of the same path?) can make a great place for intervals. And by not timing them, you make them a wee bit less serious. (You can even do untimed intervals on a track if you like.) Use distances and recovery times similar to those mentioned above for track.

There are many variations on these interval themes. You can, if you wish, designate specific portions of your road course for the record books, bring your stopwatch, and log a set of secret world's records. Earlier, I mentioned uphills. They sure do teach you to breathe deeply. Jim Ryun, former world record holder in the mile, used to run 2:30 half miles up a steep hill in his training.

Less well known are the benefits of shallow downhill intervals. Shallow downhills build speed. One coach used them to make "sub-four-minute-milers" out of his cross-country runners (most of whom were good for about 4:10 to 4:20 on a flat track). The experience increased the runners' confidence—and their leg speed—dramatically. Careful, limited use of downhill intervals can help you, too. But don't even think about this on a steep downhill. Steep downhills accentuate the pounding that can hurt you.

Interval workouts, physiologically speaking, tear your muscles down. The benefits actually come in the following days, during which you'll run slow, take easy workouts, or take rest days.

I recommend every possible luxury and precaution after an interval workout. Warm down with a nice slow jog. Stretch slowly and gently. Massage your legs after your shower. The next day, run a short course slowly and gently. When you start doing intervals, don't do more than two per week. Don't go beyond three per week until you've thoroughly outgrown this book.

Will these interval workouts teach you what racing feels like? Yes and no. Yes, they'll teach you to run fast. But in your racing you may find you can run faster still. You may, for example, finish your set of three half miles completely exhausted—but then, a week later in competition, you may do a three-mile race at the same pace you did for the intervals. Good racers can perform much better than their training times would suggest.

As I said earlier, speedwork carries with it the threat of injury. This is where the plodding joggers have a clear advantage over more frenetic runners: if you aren't trying to do your best, you have an excellent

Starting Pistols

There are two types of starting pistols commonly seen at races: the inexpensive ones, available at many discount sporting goods departments for under $20, and the ones used by real offical red-sportcoated meet directors.

The less expensive pistols are .22 caliber, the fancier ones are .32 caliber. Fine print devotees take note: rulebooks specify .22s on indoor tracks, and .32s outdoors. As a practical matter, the .22s are loud enough to use outdoors for a small race. A .32 makes an overbearing noise indoors, as one meet official showed us when he brought the wrong gun.

When I was in high school, every race was started with an official pistol. In college cross-country, pistols were rare. Coaches just shouted, "Go!" Apparently, college coaches see no need for ceremony.

chance of never getting injured.

The more anxious you are to go fast, the greater your chances of injury. Speedwork uncovers the weakest link in your muscle chain. Muscle strains occur for a variety of reasons, most of which are Latin to me, but two have been aptly explained.

The first has to do with how a muscle works. In a normal muscle, not all the fibers contract during any specific activity. The fibers are supposed to relieve each other. The "in use" motor fibers are repeatedly called upon, however, during a repeated strenuous activity. Without ample rest time to replenish themselves with oxygen, these muscle fibers fatigue. Their contractile efficiency is diminished by the accumulated metabolic slag heap. As they continue to fatigue, they reach a point where they can't contract properly. They abruptly tear instead.

It's a dreadful feeling. You can be running at race pace, feeling invincible, and then in a single stride you're reduced to limping. When I was a high school kid, a pulled muscle healed in a week. Now it takes a month.

Muscles can tear another, even less elegant, way: If you haven't done enough stretching, your muscles may be too tight for the longer stride length that faster speeds demand.

Everyone knows stretching exercises can prevent, or at least lessen the odds of, these injuries. But many people don't know the role your shoes play. Most running shoes are designed with the heel about a centimeter higher than the forefoot. Some track spikes have little or no heel lift. If you switch to track spikes only on race day, it's an enormous strain on your calf muscles. That centimeter may not feel like a big stretch, but over the course of a race at maximum effort, it's an enormous strain on your calf muscles. I used to shred my calf muscles this way every year at our conference championships. (And I thought college kids were so smart.) If you race in shoes like that, train in them. And stretch.

My last bit of injury-avoidance advice is this: don't run as hard or fast as you possibly can in interval workouts. If you think you can handle four half miles at 2:45, run them at 2:50. Or do only three instead of four. You may be completely capable of running faster—all except one little batch of muscle fibers, which need to catch up with the rest of your body's development.

This can be frustrating advice. If you're training seriously, your body will occasionally reward you with breakthrough days, when you feel invincible and tireless. You won't want to hold back. But you should. You can't tell that those few muscle fibers are suffering until it's too late. By staying healthy, you can run that fast the following week.

Sometimes your muscle gives you a warning: instead of abruptly tearing, it feels tight and sore—a localized soreness, which, with experience, you'll recognize is different from the general soreness you get from any strenuous workout. When you feel that soreness, don't run. Go hiking, cycling, swimming, rowing, or something similar. Give the muscle several days to heal, and pay close attention to it as you gingerly return to slow running.

Here's an interesting observation: most of the injuries my friends and I have sustained, we've gotten in workouts, not in races. You'd think the reckless abandon with which we race would cause many a shredded muscle, but that hasn't been my experience. Part of the reason may be that we'd often push the envelope in training to include fast quarter miles and other injury-prone workouts.

Running fast is great fun. It feels good, it amazes you, and it gives you a nice warm inner feeling. That's why it's worth so much fuss and bother.

In an ideal world, road running would be perfectly safe. In our world, it carries a few risks that only you can minimize. And now here's the good news: the behavior that minimizes the risks also has a soothing effect on you, by making you act and feel more like a person making sensible decisions, rather than a helpless adversary of all that traffic.

One of the things I do for a living is accident investigation and reconstruction, and I have studied the way the road and its laws work for runners, bicyclists, and the noisy majority, motorists. This arcane field of study has taught me some things that can help you understand some not-necessarily-obvious engineering principles that underlie safety questions.

Let's start out with a dirty little fact: the traffic environment isn't particularly well engineered for pedestrians. Motorists and bicyclists are much better off. They're both vehicle operators, and the laws and ordinary driving practices provide for easy, smooth, and fluid interactions among vehicles.

For example, a motorist doesn't have to scan a 360-degree field of view while driving his car. Normal driving practices put all potential conflicting traffic within the much smaller field of scan taught in driver's education. Another example: on roads both wide and narrow, all vehicles usually follow a simple procedure: slower traffic keep right, faster traffic pass on the left. I could go on, but you get the idea. The system provides for all sorts of contingencies in traffic situations, and vehicle operators don't have to do much creative thinking to get the system to work for them.

Now throw a runner into the picture, and that nice system can occasionally come unglued. You're not a vehicle. You don't fit into the pattern of vehicular behavior. You're supposed to be on the opposite side of the road from vehicles, and you may have to scan damn near 360 degrees to find possible conflicting traffic. On many roads, there's not enough space for you nor is there a coherent set of traffic regulations that will keep you safe. You're the odd man out.

But if you recognize the limitations of this situation, and act appropriately, you can run safely, even on some busy roads.

Let's start out with the obvious, the width problem. Most country roads are about 18 to 20 feet wide (this varies from state to state), most cars are a bit under six feet wide, and everyone wants several feet of "shy distance" beside them. Suppose you're running on the left side of the road, where you belong, and you see an oncoming motorist. You expect him to veer to his left, to leave you some room. But unbeknownst to you, there's another approaching car behind you. All it takes is a slight headwind to render that car's approach inaudible. You assume there's no traffic behind you and wonder why the motorist ahead isn't giving you space. You may even take this problem personally.

There isn't room for all three of you. The oncoming motorist is in a tight spot. A potential collision is coming at him very quickly. He can stand on his brakes and risk a skid; or stand on his horn and hope you'll step onto the shoulder for just a second; or thread his car through the tiny available space, after which you will undoubtedly salute his skilled driving with half a victory sign.

Now I'm a runner, too, and I abhor the thought of interrupting my nice fluid stride to step onto the shoulder, especially when I'm in the midst of a triumphant finishing sprint and the shoulder is overgrown with poison ivy. But under the circumstances, it's the best alternative.

The road-width problem becomes more severe under conditions of poor visibility. (These include nighttime, morning and evening when the sun is in everyone's eyes, and fog.) People need more margin for error because they can barely see where they're going.

It's a good practice to glance behind you when you see an oncoming car. You may see an overtaking car

120

that you couldn't hear, and you demonstrate to the motorist that you're looking to see what his options are. Another good practice: I often hold my right arm straight out, a gesture to claim more space. It often works (but not at night, when the arm is invisible).

Sometimes, a motorist may not give you much room, even though there's no oncoming traffic. Don't rush to accuse him of attempted homicide. He may be reluctant to make an abrupt swerve, especially if the pavement is slightly wet. He may misjudge the width of his car or be comfortable with less shy distance than you or, most likely, simply be oblivious to your needs.

Don't flatter yourself by misinterpreting that obliviousness for personal hostility. He doesn't give a hoot about you. Let him go by, and from that moment forward, don't give a hoot about him. In general, don't give in to that temptation to feel superior to everyone else, just because you're out running and they're miserable overweight slobs. That attitude generates body English, which invites confrontations you don't need. Just smile, wave, and forgive minor trespasses. The world needs less hostility.

When you're running on a narrow road, beware the blind corner. A motorist coming around that corner may have virtually no time to react to your presence. Frankly, there's no guaranteed way to compensate for this, but I can suggest two techniques that have worked for me so far. (1) As you approach a blind

corner, move away from the pavement edge to the middle of the lane. You'll become visible a few feet sooner, giving the motorist additional time to react. As soon as you see an oncoming motorist, briskly sidestep to the edge. (2) As you approach a blind corner, look ahead and behind you, and if there is no traffic in either direction, cross over to the right side of the road. After you round the corner, immediately cross back.

Now consider a less obvious hazard: the invisible reflective vest. Night is a great time for running, but it also brings hazards many people don't understand. Suppose you buy a reflective vest. If you take it into a dark room and observe it with a flashlight, you'll marvel at its brightness. And when you're out on the road, most motorists will see it from far away and react accordingly.

But don't count on it. *Under some conditions, a reflective vest doesn't reflect.* One common problem is this: car headlights are aimed at the pavement. Your vest is three to five feet in the air. The headlights may not illuminate your vest. The solution: wear reflective ankle bracelets *in addition to* the vest. You need both the vest and the ankle bracelets for two reasons: you want the greater surface area of the vest, and the ankle bracelets are concealed from view by minor rises and dips in the road. (The ankle bracelets have an additional benefit: they move, which makes them very conspicuous.)

There are many other insidious ways a reflector can

fail to perform. If the left headlight on a car is burned out, the motorist's "observation angle" (the angle subtended from the light source to the reflector and then back to the observer's eye) can be too great for the reflector to perform. (Reflector performance is tested at an unrealistically narrow observation angle of 0.2 degree.) If headlights are mis-aimed, the reflector may not be seen. If you're facing a series of oncoming cars, the first motorist may see you but the ones behind him may not. The reasons: their headlights are blocked by the car ahead, and the headlights from the lead car will not reflect your vest back to them, because the observation angle is much too large.

For these reasons, you can be decked out in an embarrassingly conspicuous costume, yet motorists might not see you until they're almost on top of you. This is not hypothetical: my own wife once didn't see me running with a reflective vest and ankle bracelets until I was about 10 yards away from her, because she was driving the third car in a series.

Fog hurts reflector performance more than it hurts other visibility parameters. That's because light has to travel twice as far through the fog for a reflector to perform. I have an informal testing range of reflectors attached to a utility pole on the street near my home. In clear weather, they're easily visible from 1,500 feet. In fog, the visibility range is about 10 percent of that. With this in mind, and because I don't trust the other guy to be properly observant, I revert to the hated basement exercise bike on foggy nights.

Also, it should go without saying, the tiny bits of reflective trim found on many running garments are inadequate. There's no substitute for lots of square inches.

Reflective accessories are made in two ways: tiny glass beads can be glued to a fabric, or a vinyl-like material can have tiny cube corner reflectors molded into it, but there is a difference: the glass beads on fabric can be made into a more attractive material, which is reasonably pleasant to wear, but the molded vinyl-like material retains its reflecting properties longer. The beaded material eventually gets so dirty that the beads don't reflect, and washing doesn't restore their reflecting power. Reflectors, unlike lights, don't warn you when they stop working. So as you use a beaded material, test its reflective properties with a flashlight. Hang the material up and walk 20 to 30 feet away from it. Hold the flashlight next to your eye and shine the flashlight at the material. The material should be brilliant. Throw the material away when its performance deteriorates.

One thing to keep in mind when you're considering your own visibility (the people in the business call it "conspicuity") is that seeing is not an orderly process. You do not automatically see something placed in front of your eyes.

You don't see with your eyes; you see with your brain. (Decades ago, experiments were conducted with blind people, in which dot matrix pictures were impressed on their backs. The test subjects were able to see simple pictures this way.) Your brain tries to make sense out of the visual data the eyes give it, and tell you what's in front of you. A motorist's brain is also occupied with the tasks of driving a car. Because the brain has its attention divided, it works slowly and makes mistakes.

Once the brain decides that it knows what's in front of you, it is very reluctant to decide that picture is wrong and "paint" a new, correct picture. The brain hangs on to the old, incorrect picture until overwhelming evidence gives you the new picture. This subject has been studied to a fare-thee-well in highway safety circles.

"One does not usually add bits and pieces to a concept [of the roadway environment when driving at night]," reports conspicuity expert Richard A. Olsen. "Rather, [the concept] is formed as a whole or Gestalt from the entire context in which information is seen. That context . . . is modified—eventually—when the accumulated information contradicting the original concept is great enough. Then, suddenly, a new Gestalt is formulated." (Transportation Research Board Circular Number 229, May 1981).

For example, have you ever been driving at night on an unfamiliar road, and discovered that the road twisted in a way different from what you'd thought only seconds earlier? Have "invisible" pedestrians and bicyclists loomed in your windshield when they were only 50 feet in front of you? You may have wondered why you didn't "see" them from 75 feet; surely they weren't completely invisible at that distance. No, they weren't, but your brain was still clinging to the view from 150 feet, when they *were* completely invisible.

This is why you may encounter strange motorist behavior at night. It's the limitations of the cognitive function of the human brain, which was designed long before today's highway system.

Your best defense against this is: anticipate that people may fail to see you; wear a garish reflectorized outfit, which will help most, but not all, of the time; and keep an eye on the shoulder, just in case you need to step there.

Finally, don't get a false sense of security when you're on a path where motorists aren't allowed. Collisions between pedestrians and bicyclists can be fatal (offhand I know of four such fatalities), and many nonfatal collisions are serious. People tend to be careless on auto-free paths, since they're "safe" from motorists. Shared-use paths can be chaotic, which is why many have strict rules governing bicyclist and pedestrian behavior.

It's lots more fun to run in the woods than it is to run on roads.

Unfortunately, cross-country running is one of running's low-profile fringes; the big, popular, publicity-grabbing events are all on pavement. The easiest places to run and find your way are on pavement. And all our lives, we've been brought about to think of pavement as the only way to get anywhere.

By contrast, running cross-country can be roughshod stuff. On a rugged course, you go slower than you could on the road because the grades are steep and the footing poor. You have to alter your stride, lifting your feet higher so you clear obstructions that could trip you. Your concentration is disrupted by looking for woodchuck holes in your path, fallen trees that weren't there last week, and muddy spots to avoid. You don't really know how long the course is, so your finishing time is meaningless except in relation to other people's times.

I think these "drawbacks" are really part of the charm. But other people apparently don't, and for that reason the sport has been excessively sanitized in much of the United States to rid it of the drawbacks.

Cross-country is primarily a school-centered sport with high school and college teams. Occasionally, you'll see an all-comers' race offered, invariably on a school's course.

Courses vary from miserable to beautiful. A miserable, sanitized course starts with a lap around the track, goes around the perimeter of the campus a few times (and if you're really sanitized, that portion will be largely on sidewalks and/or roads), and finishes with a lap around the track. These courses may even be carefully measured so you know their exact length, and your exact pace. By contrast, my favorite cross-country course of all time, at Midland School in Los Olivos, California, was simply a path through the woods. The runners never saw any sign of human handiwork, not even a fencepost or telephone pole, during the entire race. Rugged courses, especially those with logs to hurdle and streams to cross, are called European style, because that's how the Europeans design their race courses.

Like most runners, I drifted away from off-road running after I left school. Even though there were places to run off-road, they were less convenient.

But a few years ago, I saw the light. There are lots of woods around my home—why not run through them? The result is a beautiful course, clandestinely maintained by me and my machete, and occasionally shared by hunters, ATVers, the occasional dog-walking outdoorsman, and deer, foxes, skunks, raccoons, and possums.

I suggest you look for your own off-road course. It's the only way to experience running in all its primordial glory. If you live near a college or park with groomed paths, you may be in luck. No further work is necessary.

If you don't live near a ready-made course, get out your maps and look for the wooded areas nearest your home. On one of your mellow, easygoing days, go for a walk instead of a run. Walk through the woods and look for the trails. Have some pruners in your back pocket in case there are branches growing across the trails.

If you race cross-country, it's intense in a different way from road or track racing. On the road or track, your ability to master the course doesn't make a tactical difference. In a cross-country race, you can drop an opponent based on your ability to go fast over poor footing, to keep going hard and fast up a hill and accelerate over the top, and to get out of sight of an opponent, so the opponent doesn't get to copy your pace. If you're 10 or 15 seconds ahead of an opponent, you'll be out of sight in the woods, whereas on a road course, you're an open target.

And dropping opponents is important. With no opponent in sight to "key" on and a challenging, constantly undulating course, a runner is naturally inclined to slack off a tiny bit. For this reason, cross-country races often have a less even pace than road races. You start fast to establish a good position in the field and try to get away from your opponents. Then, having dropped everyone you can drop, you hang on until the finish. Physiologically, a runner who ran a more even race would have an advantage, but psychologically that runner is beaten when contact with you is lost.

Cross-country running has another small advantage: dirt surfaces absorb shock. I can run cross-country in shoes that don't absorb enough shock for road running. And because it requires a different, more deliberate high-stepping stride, it doesn't seem to produce any more sprained ankles than road running. (I still get most of my sprains on the road, where I become accustomed to perfect pavement, adjust my stride accordingly, and get injured by a pavement undulation that wouldn't give me a second thought if it were in the woods.)

For these reasons, I'd love to recommend cross-country as a way for injury-prone runners to run and avoid injury. But I can't. Only the most immaculately groomed paths are a true improvement over pavement. On all other paths, the surface is just too uneven. Steep slopes, particuarly steep downhills, can be hard on the knees.

The difference in shock absorption is nice, but today's flubber-filled shoes do a good job of minimizing shock on pavement. So that advantage is largely gone.

None of this stops me. I pay careful attention to my footing so I don't get sprains, and if I've not been running for a while, I'll go hiking for several days to strengthen my ankles before I attempt cross-country running.

If ordinary cross-country is too tame for you, how about using your wits to figure out where to go?

At an orienteering meet, you get a map and a compass. The route isn't marked.

You find your way through the woods to designated check points along the course. You pick the best route. If you're a great map reader, the best route may involve picking your way through terrain features, paralleling contour lines, and steering around knolls. If you're a great runner, the best route may be a less direct, but flatter, path.

"Very little of the event should be on trails," explains Caroline Ringo, secretary of the Delaware Valley Orienteering Association. "We keep it from being a road race. We want the thinking to be part of

it, along with the physical endurance."

Some participants are strictly noncompetitive hikers; others are deadly serious. There's a place for every level of interest and ability at most orienteering meets. Even at orienteering's national championship meet, an utter novice can walk up, pay a modest entry fee, and race against other utter novices. At that same meet, national-level contenders from all over the country will be gunning for the top spots in men's, women's, and various age categories.

An orienteering course is designed to take about an hour to run. Novice courses are about one mile long. Move out of the novice category, and you'll gradually get up to five miles. Experts may complete courses seven miles long. Overseas, some courses are even longer.

One of the great fringe benefits is the map you get to bring home after the event. Orienteering maps are ultrahigh quality—far nicer than the U.S. Geological Survey maps. They're made from new stereo aerial photos, so they're more up-to-date than the USGS maps, many of which rely on 40-year-old aerial photos. The map scale is finer (1:10,000 or 1:15,000 for orienteering, versus 1:24,000 for USGS), and there's accurate depiction of topographic features as small as fallen trees and stone walls. The maps are drawn by specialists in Scandinavia (orienteering's home, where every schoolchild is exposed to the sport) and Australia.

If an hour isn't long enough, the ultramarathon version of orienteering is called ROGAINE, or

Rugged Outdoor Group Activity Involving Navigation and Endurance. This is a team event, typically lasting six hours. But here, too, the not-so-competitive participants are welcome. Many families compete as teams and make a day's hike out of it. For the truly hard core, there are 24-hour ROGAINE events.

Even if you've never heard of orienteering, you may be surprised at how much goes on in your area. State parks, game lands, and other such lands are popular orienteering areas. It's a part of the scouting curriculum.

The single best source of information is the US Orienteering Federation, PO Box 1444, Forest Park, Georgia 30051. Send them a self-addressed stamped envelope for listings of USOF clubs and activities in your area. Then contact the nearest local club.

But don't stop your search with USOF, because not all orienteering is done by their members. Many college ROTC programs and outdoor clubs have active, non-USOF orienteering, and the ROTC has traditionally welcomed participation by folks like you, in addition to its own happy campers. Ask at local colleges about ROTC programs, and ask the ROTC officers about orienteering. Then ask park superintendents and shoe store folks. The people you meet through USOF may also direct you to non-USOF activities.

A Multidimensional Sport

The next time some boor tells you running is a one-dimensional sport, refute him with the cold hard facts. Running is colorfully diverse. Running can lead directly to your participation in, and enjoyment of:

road races
marathons and ultramarathons
cross-country races
team participation
race walking
orienteering
hiking
track races
relay races
field events
biathlons and triathlons
steeplechase and hurdles

The most dreaded bit of marathon starting-line chatter is "tales from the wall." These war stories are sufficiently chilling that they make the slightly insecure first-time marathoner feel very queasy. If you make it to the 20-mile point without suffering heatstroke, debilitating blisters, or a simple overwhelming urge to quit, your helpful competitors will tell you there's a new challenge: you feel like you've run out of gas. You just want to stop running. You've "hit the wall."

It's an awful feeling. You who ran 20 miles like a gazelle would now trade your firstborn for a La-Z-Boy. Each additional step requires Herculean effort.

The reason, metabolically speaking, is quite simple. And many runners don't know this, but proper training can make that wall *almost* disappear.

Your muscles burn two kinds of fuel: "low octane" fat and "high octane" glucose. Glucose molecules are found in three places: the muscles themselves, the bloodstream, and in your liver, where they're stored in long chains of glycogen. Fat is found—oh, never mind. *That* fat.

Glucose is in limited supply. Most runners have about two to two and one half hours of glucose supplies. The body cannot be trained to store extra glucose. Fat supplies are infinite for purposes of this discussion; even a skinny marathoner has all the fat that is needed, several times over.

Under strenuous exercise, the muscles will opt for the glucose. Now, if only you could train them to burn more of the more plentiful fat. Ah! There's the secret! (That's how bike riders make it through 12-

hour double-century rides.)

This is what specific training is all about. Long, slow workouts will train the muscles to burn fat. You see, normal low-level muscle activity burns fat. Glucose kicks in at a higher effort level, so a languid jog will burn mostly fat whereas a high-quality speed workout burns all glucose.

If you do a lot of languid jogging in training, your muscles become trained to use fat at a slightly higher speed and effort level. If that languid jog lasts long enough to partially deplete your glucose stores, it will burn still more fat. Burning fat is like any other physical activity; you get better at it if you do it more often. (That's why bike riders go out for three- and four-hour rides several times per week.)

By contrast, most of us who run six or eight miles at a pop, don't train ourselves to burn fat. Our workouts are relatively brief, and they allow the muscles to rely entirely on the liver's glycogen stores.

So you need workouts tailored specifically to fat burning. How many and how long should these workouts be? Good question, because running lots of workouts long enough to train you for fat burning may foster overuse injuries in your muscles and joints. As an extreme example, if you tried to put in the hours that bike riders put in, you'd guarantee yourself an injury. And there's no digital readout on your belly to tell you whether you're burning fat or muscle.

For these reasons, my answer is admittedly inexact. It calls for a bit of judgment on your part:

A prospective marathon runner should do some

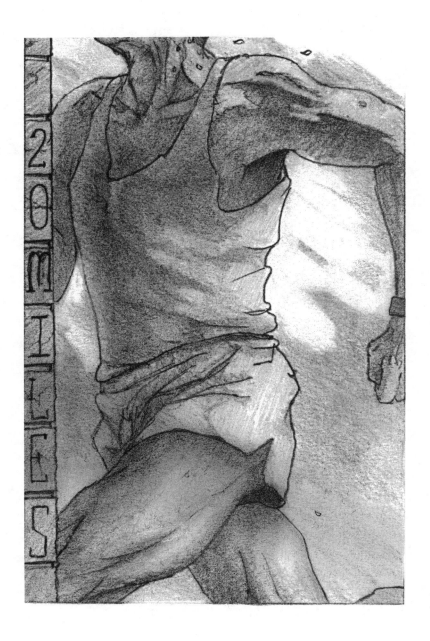

139

long workouts anyway, to accustom his muscles and bones to long-duration running. A bare minimum of three to five runs of 16 to 18 miles, deliberately run at an easygoing shuffle, is valuable preparation for race day. (Many runners think these distances are too short, and that you should run the marathon distance, or even longer, in training. Possibly they're right. Possibly they're wrong. I don't know what's right for you, but I was happy with 16-mile training runs.) The slow pace is important, because you want to get through the long workout with minimum wear and tear on your body. Your only assignment is to plod through it. These workouts are not race pace simulations.

Your last ultralong training run should be about 10 days before race day, to give you ample time to recover. Workouts of this length will certainly train you for the fat zone (18 miles at 8:00 per mile is 2:24). If you do several of these, you'll probably develop a sixth sense to feel the difference between fat-burning and glucose-burning effort levels. And eat lots of carbohydrates to restore your glycogen supply. Use sugar for a quick lift.

One way to complement your long runs is to do some lengthy hikes. A four-hour hike won't stress your bones and muscles unduly, but it will really help out in fat burning. Once again, it's a viable way for you to train for your running goals, while doing something social in the company of a nonrunner. Long bike rides may help some, too, although for the most part they exercise the wrong muscles.

My Best Friends Do Me Wrong

This is a story about dietary fat, protein, and alcohol—three delightful ingredients that make life worth living. The problem with them is that excess quantities slow you down. Eat too much fat and your body's chemical energy is diverted away from muscle motion in order to laboriously digest that fat and make it into body fat stores. The body fat stores, in turn, are the low-octane fuel that is so hard for your muscles to use.

The same is true of alcohol and protein. Alcohol is laboriously digested into fat. This slows you down three times: once when the alcohol addles your brain, a second time when it saps your energy during digestion, and the third when you have to burn fat instead of glucose. Excess protein slows you down because it, too, is laboriously digested into body fat stores. Instead of steak, eat pasta. Instead of ice cream, gorge yourself on frozen yogurt (which really tastes lots better than the name would suggest).

If you want to go fast on race day or generally feel more alert and springy, go light on these three things and steer yourself toward high-octane carbohydrates and simple sugars.

Marathon Pace

Even a seasoned runner must approach a marathon differently from shorter races. In a mere 10-miler, you feel good at the start, and you bound out fast. That kind of pace will ruin you in a marathon.

Start slow. Run at a lazy plod, slower than your hoped-for average race pace. You do this for two reasons: to make sure your muscles burn fat instead of limited glucose stores, and to warm up slowly and evenly, to forestall any possible injury.

Hold yourself back for the first 8 miles. Watch all the runners you hope to beat disappear over the distant horizon ahead. Smile craftily; you'll reel them in later on.

After 8 miles, allow yourself to crack the throttle slightly. But still hold yourself back. At the halfway point, increase your effort level some more. And around 16 to 18 miles, push the throttle all the way forward. Now, you'll naturally find the best pace you can maintain to the finish.

When you run a marathon this way, you get to pass hundreds of runners in the last 10 miles. Boy, is that a way to boost your morale!

Now that you understand the fat/glucose difference, you can use this information in many physical endeavors besides marathon running. Whether you're taking the kids for a canoe trip or helping a friend move furniture, all-day-long bouts of exercise can leave you very flat. The right diet and moderated effort level can help you avert the problem.

Every year here in Pennsylvania, ALPO Petfoods, Inc., and the Emmaus Road Runners host a slightly weird two-mile cross-country race for dogs-plus-owners. In four years, the K-9 Run has grown from 40 dogs to 83.

Well, when the going gets weird, the weird turn pro. I attend this race each year, escorting no fewer than three Siberian huskies, a dog-restraining device quite unlike conventional leashes, and old long johns for cold-weather wear. The other runners all have one dog apiece, and those trendy nylon running suits. Compared with me, they look normal. And every year, just enough of them beat me to keep me from taking home one of the prizes (50 pounds of ALPO).

Prize or no prize, running with a dog can be sheer joy, and this race is a perfect illustration why. If you can imagine 83 dogs and no dog fight, you can see how much they love running. Dogs—well, most breeds of dogs—are born runners, and they appreciate running more than people. Having a dog as your running companion can also keep you motivated and help you look forward to each workout; their enthusiasm is contagious.

When your dog is in good shape, it will challenge you with that beautiful, bounding stride. When not in shape or in hot weather, your dog will ma-and-pa you by sprinting the first half mile and then fading to a languid trot. It'll make you laugh, which is always beneficial, and it will give you the official duty of setting a sensible pace.

Unlike people, dogs never have a schedule conflict or work-related headache; nor do they get tired of your favorite route. They're the most convenient running companions, always ready to romp with you. They don't criticize your stride. They love you for running with them. Besides, what decent person doesn't love his dog and want to make the dog happy?

For these reasons, and others, dogs are running companions well worth the small amount of extra care they demand.

The extra care comes from the fact that dogs don't think for themselves. Most are such hammerheads they'll kill themselves of dehydration and heat exhaustion trying to please you. They'll run till their paws are raw and bloody. And many won't complain, even if they're in serious trouble. So you have to be careful on their behalf.

Many people have trouble controlling a dog while running. They use a conventional leash, a terrible tool for the job. You have to sacrifice your arm motion to hold the dog in check. And if your dog is pulling on its leash and trying to take off, as Siberians are famous for, there goes your nice graceful arm and leg motion.

You become distorted into a biomechanical disaster. If the dog heels obediently, you're still the loser: the leash dangles right where it can trip you. Even on a good day, I can get shoulder cramps from running with a dog on a leash.

High technology has solved all these problems. In five minutes, you can build yourself a waist-mounted dog-running harness like mine. Believe it; the harness works where a leash doesn't. Using the harness, I can control three dogs who together weigh 150 pounds, refuse to learn the "heel" command, and have the strength to pull our dogsled at 20 miles per hour.

The harness is simplicity itself. Get an old leather belt to tie around your waist at the narrowest point. Loop the handle of a short training leash (available at pet stores) around the belt. It should be just long enough to reach the floor. (Or you can use a piece of rope and some hardware store buckles to make your own short leash to tie to the belt.) Attach the buckle to your dog's collar. Add an additional rope for each additional dog.

The advantages are many. Your arms are now free to swing as they were meant to. The dog is attached to a point lower on you, so it's harder for the dog to pull you off balance. The rope is so short that it's less likely to trip you (but nothing is guaranteed, so stay alert to the rope's position). The short rope forces the dog to run right beside you. If you do need to give your dog an admonishing jerk on the leash, you can grab the rope, jerk it, and immediately return to your normal arm motion.

The other precautions for safeguarding your dog's well-being are simple enough . . . if you follow them diligently. Start out gradually, with long walks, then run the dog for a mile or two. Rest days in between running days are mandatory for a beginning dog. And even if the dog doesn't seem tired, never run it on pavement two days in a row until the paws have had lots of gradual conditioning. Inspect all paws for raw spots after *each* run, and if you see a raw spot, give the dog plenty of time to heal. And learn your lesson from the raw spot; it means you pushed the dog too far. In hot weather, keep workouts short and slow; the dog has a fur coat and can't sweat. A dog will need to drink astonishing quantities of water after running in the heat; don't let the water dish run dry.

Be on a keen lookout for problems such as arthritis and hip displasia, so you don't exacerbate them. Ask your vet if you have any doubt. Always be suspicious and imagine your dog is hurting badly, but running hard to please you. (That's a true description of many dogs, by the way.) Look for painful symptoms the dog is trying to ignore. Use my harness system to control your dog. Don't run with the dog at night; it can't be seen by others under conditions of visual clutter, and you can ill afford the added duties of herding the dog when you have such an additional challenge just to see the roadway.

Bringing the dog does increase all the usual risks of injury from falling or colliding with unwelcome traffic. Your defense against these risks is to carefully monitor the dog and its restraint system, exercise close control over the dog, and carefully observe the road or path and all traffic you encounter.

Y'all will have lots of fun together. My dogs and I sure do.

What a stupid idea, running on a treadmill.

Easy for me to say. I work for myself, and can often slip out the door for a midday run through the woods.

Many of you who work together to build civilization have less attractive options for your daily run. Your only daytime to yourself may be a 30-minute lunch hour at an office where there's no provision for employee exercise. That leaves you with 6:00 A.M., evening after the kids are in bed, or whatever else you squeeze in.

For all these reasons, indoor torture devices, including the all-important headphone stereos, were invented. If this is your lot in life, here are some pointers.

Good treadmills are very expensive. You'll probably prefer to join a club that has expensive ones, rather than spend all that money yourself. But if that's not an option, even inexpensive treadmills can be part of a good workout plan.

The key is to use your treadmill for what it's good for, and not use it for what it's bad for. No treadmill is good for long, slow distance workouts—the boredom factor is just too great when you spend 40 minutes watching the same wall. An inexpensive

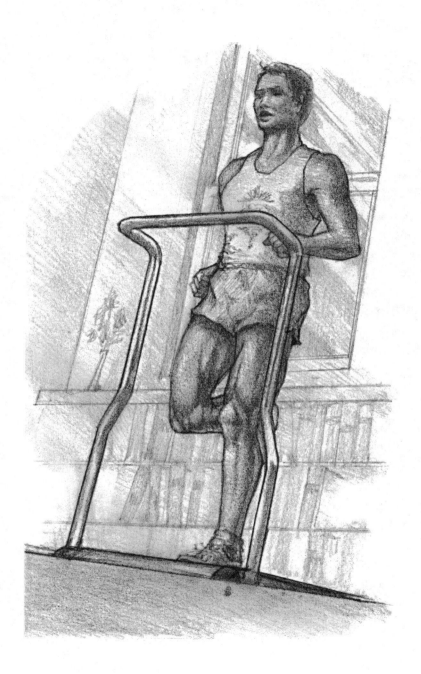

treadmill isn't good for speed workouts, because it won't go fast enough.

But all treadmills are great for walking and hill workouts, and expensive ones are good for speedwork; in fact, they have several advantages over the road and track for speedwork. And all treadmills can do excellent hill-climbing interval workouts.

Many of these advantages stem from the fact that you can run exactly the speed you set, at the uphill grade you set (if any). The treadmill is much more exact than the open road, or even the track, can ever be.

Treadmills allow you to do your warm-up and warm-down in "hill-climbing" mode. This posture lowers your heel, providing some gentle stretching during warm-up. And it lowers your leg speed during warm-up and warm-down, reducing the chances of muscle injury. (You can set the treadmill on a grade of 5 to 10 percent for this.)

Another treadmill advantage is that it's in a supervised setting. For the person in a remedial fitness program, trained help is just a shout away. (At home, you can keep a telephone nearby.)

You can run with a friend of completely different ability level. You aren't tied together, but your treadmills are next to each other.

Treadmills do mimic the open road quite well, physiologically speaking. You can train on a treadmill for racing on the road, and the muscle motions will be the same. That's not as true for other indoor machines. (Bicycles, especially, are just plain different from their indoor simulators.)

And, finally, treadmills don't have potholes; uneven, sideways-sloping pavement; swerving cars; or other such hazards. This makes them ideal for people gingerly avoiding, or recovering from, injuries. Also, treadmills don't have the curves of a track (which can aggravate injuries).

For an uphill workout, you might run quarter-mile intervals up a 6 percent grade. Most of us would be thrilled to do these in two minutes each; my treadmill consultant John Devlin does them in 90 seconds. Or do 30-second on/30-second off intervals on a 20 percent grade at a speed you can maintain for a set of 10 (it'll be somewhere between a slow walk and a slow jog). Or you might find the steepest grade you can maintain while walking three miles per hour. (For Devlin, it's 20 percent.) Do this for 20 or 30 minutes, and you've got yourself a workout excellent for cardiovascular fitness. Yet it can be safe for some people who can't run due to injury. It's also a way to get the most out of a less-than-excellent treadmill at some faraway hotel exercise room.

Whether uphill or flat, your timed intervals are exactly what you tell the machine to do. If you tell the machine to turn out 80-second quarters, that's what you get. On the track, you'll invariably do the first one in 74 seconds, in a foolish and short-lived burst of exuberance, and then slow down crazily to do the others. The treadmill doesn't let you do that; as a result, it disciplines you to perform exactly the workout you set out to do and sharpens your sense

The Calorie Bummer

If you're young and thin, and think running will keep you that way, well, let me throw some cold water on your hopes. Some people's metabolisms get awfully efficient as they get older. Every calorie not burned that day is saved for future use, and you know where it's saved.

Here's the true bummer, though: reasonable quantities of running, or any exercise, barely make a dent in your calorie consumption. Walking and running both consume approximately 100 calories per mile. A pound of fat contains 3,500 calories. There you are, almost three dozen miles to burn a pound. And that's just the first pound. And then you have to subtract the calories from the beer and/or ice cream you treat yourself to.

You can hope that regular exercise will speed up your basal metabolism, so that your now hypermetabolism (rather than the running itself) will burn off the energy stores. It works for some people, but not all.

of pace. It also lets you do high-quality speedwork in the dead of winter, when outdoor runners don't dare go fast for fear of pulling cold muscles.

By concentrating on speed and hill-climb workouts, you won't get bored. Even a fairly inexperienced gentleman jogger can mix it up on a treadmill by doing interval hill climbs, getting the cardiovascular rush that intervals provide without going fast enough to risk injury.

Just don't hang on to the hand rails. You'll be happier if you use your outdoor-style arm motion.

RACES

Women's Races

The 10 Largest U.S. Women-Only Races

Finishers	Race Name
4,487	L'eggs Mini
3,696 E	Race for the Cure-Susan B. Komen (IL)
3,271	Tufts Health Plan for Women
3,174	Race for the Cure-Susan B. Komen (TX)
2,935	Columbine Classic Women's Race
2,586	Alaska Women's Run
2,295	Nike Women's Race
1,335	Freihofer's Run for Women-Albany
1,161	Bonne Bell, Minneapolis
984	L'eggs Tune Up

E=estimate
Compiled by TACSTATS/USA, The National Center for
Long Distance Running and Race Walking Records and Research
of THE ATHLETICS CONGRESS, The National Governing Body
for Athletics in the USA.

Distance	Location
10K	New York, NY
5K	Peoria, IL
10K	Boston, MA
5K	Dallas, TX
5K	Denver, CO
10K	Anchorage, AK
8K	Washington, DC
5K	Albany, NY
10K	Minneapolis, MN
5K	New York, NY

Largest Marathons

The Largest U.S. Marathons

Finishers	Race Name
23,774	New York City
14,155	Los Angeles
11,865	Honolulu
10,893	Marine Corps
7,950	Boston
6,168	Old Style/Chicago
5,171	Twin Cities
4,199	Grandma's
3,960	Columbus
3,402	Portland
3,233	Houston Tenneco
3,177	Pittsburgh
3,098 E	Long Beach
2,961	Dallas White Rock
2,274	Detroit Free Press
2,252	Big Sur International
2,008	St. George
2,000 E	San Diego International
1,934	San Francisco

E=estimate
Compiled by TACSTATS/USA, The National Center for
Long Distance Running and Race Walking Records and
Research of THE ATHLETICS CONGRESS,
The National Governing Body for Athletics in the USA.

Location

New York, NY
Los Angeles, CA
Honolulu, HI
Washington, DC
Boston, MA
Chicago, IL
Minneapolis, MN
Duluth, MN
Columbus, OH
Portland, OR
Houston, TX
Pittsburgh, PA
Long Beach, CA
Dallas, TX
Detroit, MI
Carmel, CA
St. George, UT
San Diego, CA
San Francisco, CA

Road Races

The Largest U.S. Road Races

Finishers	Race Name
52,800 E	Examiner Bay to Breakers
51,075	Lilac Bloomsday Run
39,800	Peachtree Road Race
31,579	Crescent City Classic
27,062 E	Great Aloha Run
24,808	Bolder Boulder
23,774	New York City
18,690 E	Capitol 10,000
15,600	Manufacturers Hanover/ NYC #3
14,920	BIX
14,115	Los Angeles
13,400	Manufacturers Hanover/ NYC #2
12,901	Omaha Corporate Cup
11,865	Honolulu
11,473 E	Milwaukee Journal Al's Run
10,900 E	Manufacturers Hanover/ Chicago
10,893	Marine Corps

E=estimate

Compiled by TACSTATS/USA, The National Center for
Long Distance Running and Race Walking Records and Research

Distance	Location
12K	San Francisco, CA
12K	Spokane, WA
10K	Atlanta, GA
10K	New Orleans, LA
8.25M	Honolulu, HI
10K	Boulder, CO
MAR	New York, NY
10K	Austin, TX
3.5M	New York, NY
7M	Davenport, IA
MAR	Los Angeles, CA
3.5M	New York, NY
10K	Omaha, NE
MAR	Honolulu HI
8K	Milwaukee, WI
3.5M	Chicago, IL
MAR	Washington, DC

of THE ATHLETICS CONGRESS, The National
Governing Body for Athletics in the USA.

State Races

Largest Races in Each State

Finishers	Race Name
2,586	Alaska Women's Run
3,979	Azalea Trail Run–Mobile
553	Mountain Valley Spring
4,400 E	New Times Phoenix
52,800 E	Examiner Bay to Breakers
24,808	Bolder Boulder
7,043	Manchester Road Race
10,893	Marine Corps
907	Caesar Rodney
6,503	River Run
39,800 E	Peachtree Road Race
27,062	Great Aloha Run
14,920	BIX
3,126	Barber to Boise
10,900 E	Manufacturers Hanover/ Chicago
7,148	500 Festival Mini Marathon
8,000 E	Bank IV River Run
4,405	Kentucky Derby Festival
31,579	Crescent City Classic
9,797 E	Manufacturers Hanover/ Boston
3,029	Fritzbe's Runfest
776	Bridgton Four on the Fourth
4,329	Bobby Crim

Distance	Location
10K	Anchorage, AK
10K	Mobile, AL
10K	Hot Springs, AR
10K	Phoenix, AZ
12K	San Francisco, CA
10K	Boulder, CO
4.77M	Manchester, CT
MAR	Washington, DC
HMAR	Wilmington, DE
15K	Jacksonville, FL
10K	Atlanta, GA
8.25M	Honolulu, HI
7M	Davenport, IA
10K	Boise, ID
3.5M	Chicago, IL
HMAR	Indianapolis, IN
2M	Wichita, KS
HMAR	Louisville, KY
10K	New Orleans, LA
3.5M	Boston, MA
10K	Rockville, MD
4M	Bridgton, ME
10M	Flint, MI

5,171	Twin Cities
1,653	Hospital Hill Run
1,791	Gum Tree
2,634	Blue Cross
	Governor's Cup
3,325	Charlotte Observer
12,901	Omaha Corporate Cup
1,106	Chubb Life Run
4,199	Spring Lake
1,483	Duke City
1,445	Reno Gazette Journal Jog
23,774	New York City
6,780	Revco-Cleveland
4,122	Tulsa Run
6,167	Cascade Run-Off
10,398	Pittsburgh Great Race
2,883 E	Downtown
5,860	Cooper River
	Bridge Run
133	Coast to Coast
	Freedom Run
1,278	Expo
18,690 E	Capitol 10,000
2,008	St. George
2,252	Nissan Shamrock
479	Vermont City
51,075	Lilac Bloomsday Run
11,473	Milwaukee Journal, Al's Run
1,388	Big Boy Classic
175 E	Governor's Cup

E=estimate
Compiled by TACSTATS/USA, The National Center for
Long Distance Running and Race Walking Records and Research

MAR	Minneapolis, MN
HMAR	Kansas City, MO
10K	Tupelo, MS
5K	Helena, MT
10K	Charlotte, NC
10K	Omaha, NE
5K	Concord, N
5M	Spring Lake, NJ
HMAR	Albuquerque, NM
8K	Reno, NV
MAR	New York, NY
10K	Cleveland, OH
15K	Tulsa, OK
15K	Portland, OR
10K	Pittsburgh, PA
5K	Providence, RI
10K	Charleston, SC
8K	Brookings, SD
10K	Knoxville, TN
10K	Austin, TX
MAR	St. George, UT
8k	Virginia Beach, VA
MAR	Burlington, VT
12K	Spokane WA
8K	Milwaukee, WI
20K	Wheeling WV
5K	Cheyenne, WY

of THE ATHLETICS CONGRESS, The National
Governing Body for Athletics in the USA.

SPORT FOR LIFE

Will you be running when you're 70?

With a little luck and a little desire, yes.

The luck may or may not turn your way; any of us can develop medical conditions that simply prevent running. But:

- A sensible exercise program throughout your life will maximize your chances of being able to run at 70 or any age.
- There's a consolation prize for many nonrunners: you may well be in good enough shape to hike, swim, cycle, whatever.
- Running gives you more than memories. It teaches you the skill of working with your body. Doing it over a lifetime brings you to a level of self-understanding that you can't learn any other way. This knowledge helps you overcome your limitations, find the joy in exerting yourself, and focus your energy. With luck, you'll still apply this skill to running. Otherwise, you'll apply this skill to other activities, and you'll learn to appreciate them, too.

As you grow older, take the time to grow wiser. Learn what running can and cannot do. It's great exercise, but it lures all too many people in over their heads. They plunge into running too eagerly, rushing to fry their joints in marathons for which they are ill-trained, and from there straight to the orthopedic surgeon. *Running can't make you run sensibly.* That, you must do yourself.

165

For some, running is naturally fluid and easy. They can run forever. For others, including some of the best, it's a constant flirtation with injury. They have to be careful.

Runners who really *want* to stay with the sport until they're 70 are probably competitive, ambitious, and have high standards for themselves. Right away, they have a disadvantage over those who are content to jog a couple miles slowly now and again. "Driven" runners have to make sure they don't let ambition and perfectionism eclipse the long-term goal of maintaining a body that is still willing to run decades from now.

So let's think about the factors that keep us running.

• Go back to running's prefashionable roots. Do it because you love it, and do it your way. If your motivation comes from within, it will last longer.

• Don't reinvent the wheel. Or the shin splint. Do all the right things to avoid injuries. Seek out what others can tell you on this subject.

• Refresh yourself. Take a year or three off for bicycle touring or rock climbing or hiking or tennis or anything that appeals to you. (I took several years off for bike racing, running maybe 15 times a year during that era. I spent the next few years gradually resuming my running. Then, after a fair amount of soul searching, I found I really *needed* to return to my exercise roots.) At some point you may simply enjoy a new challenge and a new skill to learn. The challenge will be fun because you already know how

166

to focus your energy and work toward a goal one step at a time. And by the way, I'm not worried about your coming back to running. Sooner or later, you'll be back with a new appreciation for running's simple elegance. Many of my running friends have done exactly that—they've stopped running for a year, three years, five years, and come back. When I did, it felt like coming back home. The reasons were both mental and physical. I didn't want to lose touch with so many wonderful memories, and I realized that I preferred the way running exercised my body to the exercise I got from any other sport.

• Avoid routine. Refresh yourself within running. Change it around. Deliberately snub your familiar habits and expectations by running (slowly) with your children, or on a friend's new course, or by trying orienteering, or race walking, or some other tangent to the running sport.

• Sample other exercises for variety, in the same gentle, careful way I urge first-timers to approach running. You can use your fitness base from running to be better at these other sports. The newfangled cross-training shoes make a valid point, if only in an allegorical sense: variety is good. At some point between now and your 70th birthday, your body will want that variety.

• Be smooth and fluid. That's what makes running fun, poetic, lyrical. The runner who clenches his fists and pains himself is going to find a reason to quit sometime during the next few decades.

Take with you the things that make running

valuable. For me, running was first and foremost a way of reinventing myself as a far more capable human being. For others, it may be a fountain of youth, a way to combat cabin fever and depression, freedom from the doctor's nagging sermons and from fretting about one's own mortality, the focus of a new social circle, or a productive outlet for pent-up frustration. In time, it will probably be all these things for all of us. Appreciate them, treasure them, and let them motivate you. Use the sometimes clinical mindset necessary to monitor and limit what you do, so that it helps, and doesn't hurt, your body.

I'll be 70 in 2022. I'll see you on my path in the woods then.

In the meantime, may you always rejoice in the simplicity of mankind's first sport.

> The truest poetry lies
> Just now
> On a runner's rainy thighs
>
> While at his head
> White rings of breath
> Break with his stride.
>
> Winter trees, the windy cries
> Of seabirds blown inland
> Are witnesses
>
> To every move he makes.
> I wish him well
> Whatever barriers he breaks.

He runs towards a freedom
Desired by every man
But always there, ahead of him,

Freedom runs on swifter feet.
He runs with the joy of losing
Yet plucks a sweet

Gift from the air.
When he stops
The gift's no longer there.

I think that in his mind
He runs forever
Out of the green field. Now he is blind

With joy, striding a mountain path,
A morning beach
Hard from the sea's creative wrath,

A heavy suburb, a country road
Where rough welcome
Lives in his blood.

Yet even there, or anywhere,
He runs to lose.
On the winter air

Nothing can be seen
But fragile rings of white
Breaking on the green.

—Poem by Brendan Kennelly

RECORDS

World Records
(as of October 1, 1991)

These are the recognized records of the IAAF. Marks pending approval by the IAAF are denoted by "p". All walk records must be made on a track and all relay records must be made by teams composed of individuals from the same country.

Men

Race	Time	Name
100meters	9.92	Carl Lewis (USA)
	9.90p	Leroy Burrell (USA)
	9.86p	Carl Lewis (USA)
200m	19.72	Pietro Mennea (Ita)
400m	43.29	Butch Reynolds (US)
800m	1:41.73	Sebastian Coe (GB)
1,500m	3:29.46	Said Aouita (Mar)
Mile	3:46.32	Steve Cram (GBR)
3,000m	7:29.45	Said Aouita (Mar)
Steeple	8:05.35	Peter Koech (Ken)
5,000m	12:58.39	Said Aouita (Mar)
10,000m	27:08.23	Arturo Barrios (Mex)
20,000m	57:18.04	Dionisio Castro (Por)
	56:55.60p	Arturo Barrios (Mex)
1 Hour	20,944m	Jos Hermens (Hol)
	21,101mp	Arturo Barrios (Mex)

Location	Date
Seoul	09/24/88
New York	06/14/91
Tokyo	08/25/91
Mexico City	09/17/79
Zurich	08/17/88
Florence	06/10/81
W. Berlin	08/23/85
Oslo	07/27/85
Cologne	08/20/89
Stockholm	07/03/89
Rome	07/22/87
W. Berlin	08/18/89
La Fleche	03/31/90
La Fleche	03/30/91
Papendal	05/01/76
La Fleche	03/30/91

110m Hurdles	12.92	Roger Kingdom (US)
400m Hurdles	47.02	Edwin Moses (USA)
20K Walk	1:18:40.00	Ernesto Canto (Mex)
50K Walk	3:41.38.40	Raul Gonzales (Mex)
4 x 100m	37.79	France

(Max Morniere, Daniel Sangouma, Jean-Charles Trouabel, Bruno Marie-Rose)

	37.79p	Santa Monica Track Club

(Mike Marsh, Leroy Burrell, Floyd Heard, Carl Lewis)

	37.67p	USA National Team

(Mike Marsh, Leroy Burrell, Dennis Mitchell, Carl Lewis)

	37.50p	USA National Team

(Andre Cason, Leroy Burrell, Dennis Mitchell, Carl Lewis)

4 x 400m	2:56.16	United States

(Vince Matthews, 45.0; Ron Freeman, 43.2; Larry James, 43.8; Lee Evans, 44.1)

	2:56.16	United States

(Danny Everett, 43.79; Steve Lewis, 43.69; Kevin Robinzine, 44.74; Butch Reynolds, 43.94)

Best Performance

Marathon	2:06.50	B. Densimo (Eth)

Zurich	08/16/89
Koblenz	08/31/83
Bergen	05/05/84
Bergen	05/25/79
Split	09/01/90
Monaco	08/03/91
Zurich	08/07/91
Tokyo	09/01/91
Mexico City	10/20/68
Seoul	10/01/88
Rotterdam	04/17/88

Women

Race	Time	Name
100m	10.49	Florence Griffith Joyner (US)
200m	21.34	Florence Griffith Joyner (US)
400m	47.60	Marita Koch (GDR)
800m	1:53.28	Jarmila Kratochvilova (Tch)
1,500m	3:52.47	Tatyana Kazankina (URS)
Mile	4:15.61	Paula Ivan (Rom)
3,000m	8:22.62	Tatyana Kazankina (URS)
5,000m	14:37.33	Ingrid Kristiansen (Nor)
10,000m	30:13.74	Ingrid Kristiansen (Nor)
100m Hurdles	12.21	Yordanka Donkova (Bul)
400m Hurdles	52.94	Marina Stepanova (URS)
4 x 100m	41.37	German Dem. Republic (Silke Moller, Sabine Rieger, Ingrid Auerswald, Marlies Gohr)
4 x 400m	3:15.17	Soviet Union (Tatyana Ledovskaya, 50.12; Olga Nazarova, 47.82; Maria Pinigina, 49.43; Olga Bryzgina, 47.78)
5K Walk	20:17.19	Kerry Saxby (Aus)
	20:07.52p	Beate Anders (GDR)
10K Walk	41:46.21	Nadezhda Ryashkina (URS)

Best Performance

Marathon	2:21.06	Ingrid Kristiansen (Nor)

Location	Date
Indianapolis	07/16/88
Seoul	09/29/88
Canberra	10/06/85
Munich	07/26/83
Zurich	08/13/80
Nice	07/10/89
Leningrad	08/26/84
Stockholm	08/05/86
Oslo	07/05/86
Stara Zagora	08/20/88
Tashkent	09/17/86
Canberra	10/06/85
Seoul	10/01/88
Sydney	01/14/90
Rostock	06/23/90
Seattle	07/24/90
London	04/21/85

Unofficial World Road Running
Best Performances and Records

as Compiled by TACSTATS/USA as of May/June 1991

Men

Race	Time	Name
50K	2:50:55★	Don Paul (USA)
100K	6:28:11p	Don Ritchie (GBR)
10Miles	46:13	Greg Meyer (USA)
50M	4:50:51	Bruce Fordyce (GBR)
100M	1:46:38★	Yiannis Kouros (Gre)
1,000M	250:35:18★	Yiannis Kouros (Gre)
24 hr	286,463m p	Yiannis Kouros (Gre)

★ unvalidatable

Women

Race	Time	Name
50K	3:13:51	Janis Klecker (USA)
100K	7:47:29	Marcy Schwam (USA)
	7:26:52p	Birgit Lennartz (FGR)
10M	51:47	Cathy O'Brien (USA)
50M	5:59:26	Marcy Schwam (USA)
	5:40:18p	Ann Trason (USA)
100M	13:55:02	Ann Trason (USA)
24 hr	230,273m	Ann Trason (USA)
	237,861m p	Eleanor Adams (GBR)

E=estimate
Compiled by TACSTATS/USA, The National Center for
Long Distance Running and Race Walking Records and Research

Location	Date
New York	11/06/82
Spain	09/25/82
Washington, DC	03/27/83
Illinois	10/14/84
New York	11/08/84
New York	05/20/88
New York	09/28/85

Location	Date
Florida	12/17/83
Spain	09/19/81
West Germany	09/30/89
Michigan	08/26/89
Illinois	10/03/82
Texas	02/23/91
New York	09/17/89
New York	09/17/89
Great Britain	02/04/90

of THE ATHLETICS CONGRESS, The National
Governing Body for Athletics in the USA.

American Records
(As of October 1, 1991)

These are the recognized records of The Athletics Congress.

Men

Race	Time	Name
100m	9.92	Carl Lewis
	9.90p	Leroy Burrell
	9.86p	Carl Lewis
200m	19.75	Carl Lewis
	19.75	Joe DeLoach
400m	43.29	Butch Reynolds
800m	1:42.60	Johnny Gray
1,500m	3:29.77	Sydney Maree
Mile	3:47.69	Steve Scott
Steeple	8:09.17	Henry Marsh
5,000m	13:01.15	Sydney Maree
10,000m	27:20.56	Mark Nenow
MAR	2:10.04	Pat Petersen
110m Hurdles	12.92	Roger Kingdom
400m Hurdles	47.02	Edwin Moses
20K Walk	1:24.50	Tim Lewis
50K Walk	4:12.45 Ot	Dan O'Connor
	3:56.55 rd	Marco Evoniuk
4 x 100m	37.83	Olympic Team
		(Sam Graddy, Ron Brown, Calvin Smith, Carl Lewis)
	37.79p	Santa Monica TC

Location	Date
Seoul	09/24/88
New York	06/14/91
Tokyo	08/25/91
Indianapolis	06/19/83
Seoul	09/28/88
Zurich	08/18/88
Koblenz	08/28/85
Cologne	08/25/85
Oslo	07/07/82
Koblenz	08/28/85
Oslo	07/27/85
Brussels	09/05/86
London	04/23/89
Zurich	08/16/89
Koblenz	08/31/83
Seattle	05/07/88
Irvine	11/19/83
Seoul	09/30/88
Los Angeles	08/11/84
Monaco	08/03/91

(Mike Marsh, Leroy Burrell,
Floyd Heard, Carl Lewis)
37.67p   National Team
(Mike Marsh, Leroy Burrell,
Dennis Mitchell Carl Lewis)
37.50p   National Team
(Andre Cason, Leroy Burrell,
Dennis Mitchell, Carl Lewis)

4 x 400m   2:56.16   Olympic Team
(Vince Matthews, 45.0; Ron Freeman,
43.2; Larry James, 43.8; Lee Evans, 44.1)
2:56.16   Olympic Team
(Danny Everett, 43.79; Steve Lewis,
43.69; Kevin Robinzine, 44.74; Butch
Reynolds, 43.94)

Women

Race	Time	Name
100m	10.49	F. Griffith Joyner
200m	21.34	F. Griffith Joyner
400m	48.83	Valerie Brisco
800m	1:56.90	Mary Slaney
1,500m	3:57.12	Mary Slaney
Mile	4:16.71	Mary Slaney
3,000m	8:25.83	Mary Slaney
5,000m	15:00.00	PattiSue Plumer
10,000m	31:35.30	Mary Slaney

Zurich	08/07/91
Tokyo	09/01/91
Mexico City	10/20/68
Seoul	10/10/88

Location	Date
Indianapolis	07/16/88
Seoul	09/29/88
Los Angeles	08/06/84
Bern	08/16/85
Stockholm	07/26/83
Zurich	08/21/85
Rome	09/07/85
Stockholm	07/03/89
Eugene	07/16/82

	31:28.92p	Francie Larrieu-Smith
MAR	2:21.21	Joan Samuelson
100m Hurdles	12.61	Gail Devers
	12.61p	Jackie Joyner-Kersee
	12.48p	Gail Devers-Roberts
400m Hurdles	53.37	Sandra Farmer Patrick
4 x 100m	41.61	National Team

(Alice Brown, Diane Williams,
Chandra Cheeseborough, Evelyn Ashford)

41.55p   National Team

(Alice Brown, Diane Williams,
Florence Griffith, Pam Marshall)

4 x 400m   3:15.51   Olympic Team

(Denean Howard, 49.82; Diane Dixon,
49.17; Valerie Brisco, 48.44; Florence
Griffith Joyner, 48.08)

10K Walk	46:10.26	Debbi Lawrence
	46:06.36p	Debbi Lawrence
	45:28.40p	Debbi Lawrence

p-pending approval

Austin	04/04/91
Chicago	10/20/85
Los Angeles	05/21/88
San Jose	05/28/88
Berlin	09/10/91
New York	07/23/89
Colo. Springs	07/03/83
West Berlin	08/21/87
Seoul	10/01/88
Minneapolis	07/3/90
New York	0 6/13/91
Los Angeles	07/19/91

A RUNNER'S GUIDE TO
25 GREAT CITIES OF THE WORLD

Peter Oliver is a New York freelancer who writes frequently about sports and travel. Lydia Chang is a New York-based fitness consultant who manages her own firm, Fitness Consultant Management.

Sports—not watching them but *doing* them—are usually not among the marquee attractions of city life. London, New York, Paris, or Tokyo do not leap to mind when one thinks of bike riding, hiking, or golf. And for those sports that cities can accommodate, expense and logistics often make them more trouble than they're worth.

Take basketball, for example—"the city game," as it's sometimes called. Getting accepted into a pickup game on the cement courts of New York or Los Angeles can be as difficult as admission to an exclusive men's club. Or consider racquet sports: tennis, racquetball, squash. In many cities, you must pay upwards of $50 for an hour of court time. And when you spend your first 15 minutes caught in a traffic jam—well, you're more than likely to leave your racquet home.

Thank goodness, then, for running. So simple. No need of cumbersome equipment, vast open spaces, or large blocks of time. Just a half hour, a pair of running shoes, and a will to move.

Running offers a unique escape from the city's

phantom bonds—the static confinement of car seats, elevators, office desks, conference rooms, store aisles, hotel rooms. It adds a new perspective to the city experience: it sets the city in motion. And it's *free,* a notion one barely dares to trust.

With that, here's a guide to the best running in 25 of the world's greatest cities. A place you can turn to for local running information is included in the "Resources" section of each city; note, however, that addresses and phone numbers for local running clubs have a habit of changing frequently. If you have a problem tracking down any of the U.S. running clubs, try calling the Road Runners Club of America (tel.: 703/836-0558) for the latest information.

Atlanta

The recreational soul of the city is Piedmont Park, about 2 miles north of midtown. It's the finishing area for the annual Peachtree Classic, one of the country's premier 10K road races.

The best way to reach the park from the midtown area is to head north on Piedmont Avenue. Three attractions of Piedmont Avenue: the infrequency of intersections, the wide sidewalk, and the few small hills to wake up the legs on an early morning run.

If you'd prefer to concentrate your running time in the park, catch a bus there: the southern boundary begins at 14th Street. One way to estimate the distance and decide whether you're ready to run or ride is to look for the new IBM Tower, the

Gothic/postmodern building visible from midtown. It's near the park.

The main park running loop isn't long—only about a mile—but it's pretty, circling a small lake and a ball field. It's also pretty flat, so if you want to get some hill miles in your legs, you'll probably want to make the Piedmont Avenue run as well. Most important, the park loop is well shaded, a great blessing when the summer swelter descends on Atlanta.

One other option for runners looking for hillier action is the 2-mile cross-country course at Emory University, about 5 miles northeast of the midtown area. The running path begins at the President's Estate driveway on Clifton Road and continues through the campus and Druid Hills.

Resources
General information: Atlanta Convention & Visitors' Bureau, 233 Peachtree St. NE, Suite 2000, Atlanta, GA 30303, tel.: 404/521-6688.

Route and event information: The Atlanta Track Club, 3097 E. Shadowlawn Ave., Atlanta, GA 30305, tel.: 404/231-9065.

Boston

Long before distance running became the rage of the '70s and '80s—before there were such things as running magazines, professional marathoners, and companies raking it in from the sale of running shoes—there was the Boston Marathon. Put another way, running is something of a Boston tradition, and, in such a college-infested city, there are plenty of healthy young bodies to carry the tradition forward. Even a few hotels get in on the act by providing running maps free.

OK—so you're not keen on running the entire 26-plus miles of the marathon. The route might be famous, but there are better places to run, anyway, such as the running paths on both sides of the Charles River.

The best place to start your Charles River run is near Harvard Bridge, where steps lead down from Massachusetts Avenue to the running path. Depending on which bridges you choose to cross (the Longfellow, River Street, or Eliot bridges), you can come up with anywhere from a 4- to 10-mile run. You can pace yourself with oarsmen along the river; rowing is another of Boston's aerobophilic traditions.

Another popular—and shorter—run loops the contiguous Boston Common and Public Gardens. You can be assured of two things along the 1.5-mile circuit: shade and company. It's an easy and centrally located loop—just the place for popping out of an office-bound meeting for a quick, lunch-hour or after-work run.

Resources
General information: Greater Boston Convention and Visitors Bureau, Box 490, Prudential Tower, Suite 400, Boston, MA 02199, tel.: 617/536-4100.

Route and event information: Bill Rogers Running Center, 353-T N. Marketplace, Boston, MA 02109, tel.: 617/723-5612.

Chicago

When last we tuned in to America's marathon wars, the Chicago Marathon ranked right up there in stature with its counterparts in Boston and New York. The Chicago organizers made their mark in big-time marathoning in a way befitting the financial capital of the Midwest—they offered big prize money (and appearance money) to attract the world's best.

Of course, you don't have to be among the world's best to enjoy running in Chicago. The city has two terrific running routes: Lakeshore Path and Lincoln Park. Lakeshore Path, 18 miles long from the South Shore Cultural Center north to Hollywood Beach, is the more scenic, with the lake on one side and the city on the other. It's most easily reached from downtown Chicago via pedestrian underpasses off Pearson Street, near the Hancock Tower. The northern sections of the path are best; the southern part is considered less safe.

The Lakeshore Path, however, has its drawbacks. For one thing, it's a paved path that runners must share with cyclists. For another, the scenic, lakeside setting can be frigid in the winter winds. The 5-mile cinder track in Lincoln Park is more weather-protected and cycle-resistant; a paved bike path runs alongside.

189

Resources
General information: Chicago Office of Tourism, 806 N. Michigan Ave., Chicago, IL 60611, tel.: 312/280-5740.

Route and event information: Chicago Area Runners Association, Box 47824, Chicago, IL 60647, tel.: 312/666-9836.

Dallas

Dallas is a city with a curiously indoor mentality. Many of its crisply modern downtown buildings are connected by indoor walkways and skyways, and much of its social life centers around shopping malls that encircle the city. It's the sort of town where aerobophiles are more likely to be found working out on treadmills and stair machines at health clubs—of which there are many in the Dallas area—than running outdoors.

This indoor-ness might be a result of the city's youth—it has grown up in the era of controlled environments—or an understandable response to the Texas heat, which can come on fiercely in summer. Whatever the reason, it sometimes seems to be carried a bit too far.

About the only place to run in the downtown area is along Turtle Creek, which meanders through commercial areas and along some of the prettiest residential streets in the city. Alas, traffic and numerous intersections make this route less than ideal.

The best running in Dallas can be found at White Rock Lake, about 8 miles northeast of downtown.

The distance around the lake is about 9 miles along a paved, tree-shaded path, the terrain a mix of flats and a few short hills.

Resources
General information: Dallas Convention & Visitors Bureau, 1201 Elm St., Dallas, TX 75270, tel.: 214/746-6600.

Route and event information: Inside Texas Running, 9514 Bristlebrook Dr., Houston, TX 77083, tel.: 713/498-3208.

Honolulu

Climate, scenery, and variety of terrain—the sorts of things that make Hawaii one of the most pleasant places to visit make Honolulu one of the most enjoyable cities in the world to run in. Many people do just that, so you can expect plenty of running company, along with the support of the Department of Parks and Recreation, which publishes a brochure of more than 20 running routes.

That said, the best-known district of Honolulu, the Waikiki beach area, is probably the worst for running, given its congestion of automotive and pedestrian traffic. There are, however, a couple of good areas for running on the eastern and western flanks of the Waikiki area: Kapiolani Park to the east, and, farther east, Diamond Head. A 1.8-mile triangular loop around the park (using Monsarrat, Paki, and Kapahulu avenues) is relatively flat and comes with oceanside views. For longer, somewhat hillier terrain, try the 4.6-mile loop around Diamond Head, along Monsarrat

Avenue and Diamond Head Road.

Ala Moana Park, to the west of the Waikiki area, is also fine for running. The entrance is across from the Ala Moana shopping center. There is a 2-mile loop in the park that can be extended by a mile by running around the perimeter of Magic Island.

Resources

General information: Hawaii Visitors Bureau, 2270 Kalakaua Ave., 8th floor, Honolulu, HI 96815, tel.: 808/923-1811.

Route and event information: Honolulu Department of Parks and Recreation, 690 S. King St., Honolulu, HI 96813, tel.: 808/527-6343. The Running Room, 768 Kapahulu Ave., Honolulu, HI 96813, tel.: 808/737-2422.

Houston

Houston can be a brute to runners. It's a city that air-conditioning made possible; summer survival here revolves around hopscotching from one air-conditioned environment to the next to escape the heat and humidity. Unfortunately, it's pretty hard to run using that same strategy, so running is usually best as an early morning or late-day affair.

The most convenient running route in the downtown area is along Buffalo Bayou. Paved paths running along either side of the bayou make a 4.7-mile round trip if you start at Walker Street and head west toward the turnaround point at Shepherd Bridge. Working up and down the banks of the bayou, the paths provide a variety of terrain that the Houston geography generally lacks. Take advantage of the water fountain at the far end of Shepherd Bridge, especially on a hot day.

The drawback to running along Buffalo Bayou is the bicycle traffic with which you must share the path. Similar encounters won't happen along the 3-mile, runners-only, wood-chip-covered trail around the golf course in Memorial Park, about 4 miles west of the downtown area. There is a similar, round-a-golf-course run at Hermann Park, several miles south of downtown near Rice University.

Resources
General information: Houston Convention & Visitors Bureau, 3300 Main St., Houston, TX 77002, tel.: 713/523-5050.

Route and event information: Inside Texas Running, 9514 Bristlebrook Dr., Houston, TX 77083, tel.: 713/498-3208.

Los Angeles

Los Angeles has redefined the word "city." "Metro-sprawl" might be more like it. For visiting runners the question is less about where to *run* than where to *stay* without needing to drive someplace *else* for a run. For most people the answer is Santa Monica.

Palisades Park, a mile-and-a-half-long stretch of green atop the cliffs that rise up behind the beach from the Santa Monica Pier to San Vicente Boulevard, is a favorite of runners. The park's 3-mile loop offers a variety of surfaces—dirt, grass, and concrete—a vista of the beach, a fresh ocean breeze, and shade, fittingly provided by palm trees. South of the pier, at beach level, a concrete boardwalk/bikeway winds nearly 20 miles through Venice, Marina Del Rey, and down to Redondo Beach. It is a bikeway, however, with cyclists and skaters whizzing by. Of course, for those who like running on sand, the beach is always a ready alternative.

The Hollywood Reservoir, just east of Cahuenga Boulevard in the Hollywood Hills, is a favorite spot for local runners, with its 3.2-mile asphalt path around the reservoir, and view of the famous Hollywood sign. Within hilly Griffith Park, Crystal Springs Drive, from the main entrance at Los Feliz to the Zoo, is a relatively flat 5 miles, and the ranger station about a mile in can offer advice on other routes. Circle Drive, around the perimeter of UCLA in Westwood, provides a 2.5-mile run through academia, LA-style.

Resources
General information: Greater Los Angeles Visitor & Convention Bureau, 515 S. Figueroa, Los Angeles, CA 90071, tel.: 213/624-7300. Visitor Information Center (in the Hilton Hotel), 695 S. Figueroa, Los Angeles, CA 90071, tel.: 213/689-8822.

Route and event information: City Sports Magazine, 215 Long Beach Blvd., #606, Long Beach, CA 90802, tel.: 310/437-8822.

Miami

Given all the other sports that southern Florida is known for—golf, tennis, deep-sea fishing—one doesn't think of Miami as much of a runner's city. Yet the Miami Runners Club is an active bunch, and if you don't mind the city's semitropical climate (i.e., humidity) you can have a pretty good time running around town.

One of the most popular routes is the 13-mile stretch from Parrot Jungle (11000 SW 57th Ave., South Miami) to Key Biscayne. That might sound long, but the flatness of the terrain makes the going relatively easy. Do the complete round trip and—yes—you've run the full marathon distance. The best time to make the run is Saturday, when Miami Runners Club members are stationed along the way to hand out water.

Tropical Park, just more than 2 miles west of Coral Gables, is another fine place to run—with runs of up to 5 miles possible on the park's paved roadway. If you're a crack-of-dawn type of runner (and early morning is the best time to run in Miami), you might want to run along the cart paths in one of the many golf courses in the area. Check with the golf-course pros first; they're likely to be accommodating as long as you don't interfere with the golfers.

Resources
General information: Visitors Services, Greater Miami Convention and Visitors Bureau, 701 Brickell Ave., Suite 2700, Miami, FL 33131, tel.: 800/283-2707.

Route and event information: Miami Runners Club, 7920 SW 40th St., Miami, FL 33155, tel.: 305/227-1500.

New Orleans

Exercise, *any* exercise, is essential for anyone spending time in New Orleans. That's because New Orleans is an epicurean dream and a dietary nightmare—an irresistable invitation to gastronomic overindulgence, what with all its deep-fried beignets, gumbo, oysters, blackened fish, and fire-breathing Cajun martinis. So go ahead and eat; it's the first commandment of New Orleans. Then don your running shoes and make use of all those newly consumed calories.

Perhaps the best street route to run in the downtown area is along St. Charles Avenue, which makes a 5-mile arc from the French Quarter to Carrollton Avenue. St. Charles Avenue is best known for stately homes and its old, wood-sided trolley cars. If you maintain a good pace, you may well outrun the trolley. Most runners will zip along the wide grassy median strip that the trolley tracks are set in, although the avenue's sidewalks are well-shaded—a welcome feature given the heat and humidity that beset the city in summer.

Audubon Park, about 4.5 miles along St. Charles Avenue from the downtown area, is another good place to run. A 1.8-mile asphalt path that circles a golf course and lagoon can be combined with a 1.5-mile loop (also asphalt) around the zoo, just across Magazine Street from the park. A good New Orleans running strategy: make the run up St. Charles Avenue, through the park and the zoo, then cool down by riding the trolley for much of the trip back to the

French Quarter. An alternative, if you want to get out of the center of the city, is to run the 2.5-mile route through the lower portion (south of I-610) of City Park, about 3 miles north of downtown.

Resources
General information: New Orleans Tourist and Convention Commission, 1520 Sugar Bowl Dr., New Orleans, LA 70112, tel.: 504/566-5031.

Route and event information: New Orleans Track Club, Box 52003, New Orleans, LA 70152, tel.: 504/482-6682.

New York

What a shame it is that Central Park is saddled with such a lurid reputation. New Yorkers can tell you that the park is the place to find sanctuary from the pressures of city life, and it is certainly the place to run (although you can run along the East River above 60th Street, as well as along the Hudson River in Riverside Park).

There are two basic running routes in Central Park: the 1.6-mile circuit of the reservoir (best entrance: 90th Street and 5th Avenue) and the main loop of just more than 6 miles around the park's perimeter. If rubbing sweaty elbows with the rich and famous is your thing, make a couple of early morning reservoir laps: you're likely to be in the company of well-known actors and New York power-brokers.

The Loop (as the outer circuit is known) is closed to vehicular traffic on weekends and during some nonrush-hour times on weekdays, but an inner lane is reserved at all times for runners and cyclists. On weekends, running the Loop is perfectly safe, save for the danger imposed by cyclists and the growing ranks of in-line roller skaters. The terrain is generally rolling, with just one major hill at the northern end of the park.

Running the outer loop at off hours is probably not a good idea (even if the roadway is lit), especially in northern sections of the park. By cutting across at 72nd Street, it's possible to make a shorter, 1.7-mile loop and stick to the park's safer, southern end.

Resources
General information: New York Convention and Visitors Bureau, 2 Columbus Circle, New York, NY 10019, tel.: 212/397-8222.

Route and event information: New York Road Runners Club, 9 E. 89th St., New York, NY 10128, tel.: 212/860-2280.

Philadelphia

Given that Fairmount Park is more than five times the size of New York's Central Park, Philadelphia is perhaps the premier northeastern city to run in, with runs of 10 miles or more possible without crossing a major intersection. That this runner's bounty is largely unknown outside Philadelphia can be blamed on three things. One, the best-known running route in Philadelphia—Sly Stallone's jaunt through the Italian Market and up the art-museum steps in *Rocky*—has almost nothing to do with the city's best places to run. Two, Philadelphia does not have an internationally famous marathon, à la Boston or New York. And, three, most things worth knowing about Philadelphia are largely unknown outside Philadelphia.

So for the best running in the city, start at a familiar reference point—the art-museum steps. From there, head down toward the boat docks (where you'll usually find rowers in the early morning) and Kelly Drive (formerly the East River Drive).

A loop of more than 6 miles can be made by following the drive north to Falls Bridge, crossing the bridge, and returning south along the West River Drive. The riverside running is pretty flat, but runners who want to test their hill power can try the steep (in some cases, very steep) roads that climb eastward toward Germantown from Kelly Drive.

Resources
General information: Philadelphia Convention and Visitors Bureau, 1515 Market St., Philadelphia, PA 19102, tel.: 215/636-3300 or 800/537-7676.

Route and event information: Northeast Roadrunners of Philadelphia, 3904 I St., Philadelphia, PA 19124, tel.: 215/535-7335.

Phoenix

According to the National Oceanographic and Atmospheric Administration, Phoenix has more clear days and fewer cloudy days than any other city in the United States. Phoenix is surely one of the best cities in the country for winter running, as the typically clear days of January, with temperatures in the 60s, are a runner's dream.

That's the good news. The not-so-good-news is that the midday heat of summer can be unrelenting and even dangerous for runners. This is, after all, the desert, where 110° in the shade isn't uncommon and where shade itself is uncommon. The blessing is that the heat, untrapped by humidity, can dissipate quickly after sunset, often dropping 30 degrees or more at night. Early morning and late-evening runs can be pleasant enough, even in summer.

Phoenix has many parks, a fact that sounds better for runners than it actually is. The parks tend to feature desert and mountain terrain great for such activities as hiking, picnicking, rock climbing, and horseback riding, but not so great for running. Of course, you can run in a park such as South Mountain Park, but trail surfaces can be uneven and the terrain hilly, and encounters with hikers and horseback riders are likely.

So what's left for runners? Probably the most popular route among locals is along the Arizona Canal, which wends through the northern part of the city. The canal route is roughly 24 miles long and relatively flat. But take warning, especially in this desert world: There are no water fountains along the way.

Resources
General information: Phoenix and Valley of the Sun Convention and Visitors Bureau, 1 Arizona Ctr., 400 E. Van Buren St., Suite 600, Phoenix, AZ 85004, tel.: 602/254-6500.

Route and event information: Arizona Road Racers Club, Box 37876, Phoenix, AZ 85069-7876, tel.: 602/954-8341.

San Diego

Sports Illustrated once named San Diego "the sports and fitness capital of the U.S." Although similar titles have been bestowed on Boulder, Colorado, and Seattle, there's little doubt that San Diego's perfect climate (not too hot, not too cold) and a setting that brings together mountains and the sea—not to mention an enthusiastic populace—make it one of those rare cities where athletic recreation is a big attraction for visitors. This is not only a city to run in but a city to run in *competitively;* you can count on finding some race somewhere in the San Diego area virtually any weekend of the year.

Here, runners can choose between the flatter routes along harbors, bays, and beaches, and hillier routes in the canyons. For flat terrain, Mission Bay, northwest of downtown, is the most popular area. Loops of up to 5 miles are possible on the wide sidewalks along West Mission Bay Drive, Mission Boulevard, and Pacific Bay Drive. A bonus is that at almost any point you can veer off the sidewalk and rest in the tree-dotted fields leading down to the bay, take in the sea breezes and watch the boats go by.

For a taste of canyon-style running, Balboa Park, just north of downtown, is the place to go. The 1,400-acre park has a seemingly endless, complex weave of roads and trails, with plenty of ups and downs. Most runners prefer the portion of the park west of Park Boulevard, along routes that take them past the various museums. The park is also home to the San Diego Zoo, so if the hills get to your legs and lungs, you can always drop back to a leisurely stroll among the animals.

Resources
General information: San Diego Visitor Information Center, 2688 East Mission Bay Dr., San Diego, CA 92109, tel.: 619/276-8200.

Route and event information: Race Place, tel.: 619/485-9806.

San Francisco

In running circles, San Francisco is perhaps best known for the annual 7.5-mile Bay to Breakers race, an event that's about one part race and three parts masquerade-in-motion (the winner is often less remembered than runners' outrageous attire or stunts).

San Francisco is known for its hills—a challenge for even the fittest of runners. Luckily, the generally cool climate and—of course—the fog helps prevent overheating in the midst of a run over the city's precipitous ups and downs.

However, not *all* of San Francisco is relentlessly hilly. The most popular—and relatively flat—place to run is Golden Gate Park, a profusion of cultural, recreational, and botanical attractions compressed into 1,000 acres, designed by Frederick Law Olmsted, and a recognizable cousin of his earlier work on New

York's Central Park. On Sundays, some park roads are closed to vehicular traffic, and the park comes alive with recreational activity. In addition to an intricate network of roadways and paths that runners share with bicyclists, skaters, and strollers, there are two oval tracks near the Polo Field, and another in Kezar Stadium at the eastern end of the park.

Another popular spot for running is the 7-mile route around Lake Merced, a couple of miles south of Golden Gate Park. For a more romantic run along the beach—San Francisco running at its flattest—there is the 3-mile stretch of Ocean Beach between Cliff House and the zoo.

Resources
General information: San Francisco Convention and Visitors Bureau, Hallidie Plaza, 900 Market St., San Francisco, CA 94102, tel.: 415/974-6900.

Route and event information: City Sports Magazine, Box 193693, San Francisco, CA 94119, tel.: 415/546-6150.

Seattle

Among the citizens of Seattle, the zeal for outdoor activity approaches a secular religion, and, given the wealth of opportunity, it's easy to understand why. Look one way, from the city to the mountains, for hiking, climbing, and skiing; look another way, toward the sea, for sailing, sailboarding, and fishing. And, within the city itself, there are several good places to run, along with many other runners who put the paths to good use.

If you think of running as social activity as well as exercise, the place to go is Green Lake, about a mile north of the downtown area via Highway 99. The 3-mile loop around the pretty lake sees plenty of action, and not just from runners. On weekends especially, the Green Lake shores are taken over by runners, casual cyclists, roller skaters, mothers with baby strollers, and singles who are out to meet each other.

If you prefer a longer run, try the 12-mile Burke-Gilman Trail that at one time was a rail line. Start at the University of Washington and run northeast to Bothell, but be prepared to share the trail with cyclists.

In addition to its outdoors spirit, Seattle is also known for its damp weather, so be ready to run in rain or fog. However, despite the nearby mountains (about 40 miles east of the city) that gather snow in the colder months, Seattle's winter climate—given its northerly latitude—is relatively mild, and it is unusual to encounter snow in the city.

Resources
General information: Seattle/King County Convention & Visitors' Bureau, 1 Convention Pl. (at the corner of Union & 7th), Seattle, WA 98101, tel.: 206/461-5800.

Route and event information: Seattle Parks Department, Recreation Information Office, 5201 Green Lake Way N, Seattle, WA 98103, tel.: 206/684-4075.

Washington, D.C.

Washington was a planned city from its inception, although the master plan—with the Capitol as a hub from which major avenues radiate—was conceived before the invention of the automobile and the traffic jam. And, while the design may not have worked to the advantage of motorists, it produced distinct benefits for runners.

Wide-open spaces—specifically the Mall and the banks of the Potomac River—were part of the original lay out, providing a suitable setting for Washington's major monuments and memorials. Clean air, due to a lack of industry, along with a general feeling of openness, a result of severe height restrictions mandated in the Capitol's construction, are additional bonuses for runners.

How best to make use of the open space? The ultimate sight-seeing run is the 4-mile loop around the Mall, the 2-mile-long open area that stretches from the Capitol past the Washington Monument to the Lincoln Memorial. There are relatively few intersections to interrupt your run, although you might find yourself having to elbow through crowds of camera toters during the height of the summer tourist season.

If you run an extra mile and a half or so, you can also connect with the loop around the Tidal Basin, setting for the famous blossoming of the cherry trees in spring. And, if your legs allow, you can go farther still, through West Potomac Park to East Potomac Park, which juts out into the confluence of the Potomac and Anacostia rivers. The 4-mile loop around the park is flat and relatively shadeless, although breezes off the river can keep things reasonably cool.

Resources
General information: Washington D.C. Convention and Visitors Association, 1455 Pennsylvania Ave., Washington, DC 20005, tel.: 202/789-7000.

Route and event information: DC Road Runners Club, Box 545, McLean, VA 22101, tel.: 703/241-0395.

ASIA

Hong Kong

Given the fast pace of commercial and business activity in Hong Kong, you might be surprised to discover that the Hong Kong Running Clinic leads a run every Sunday and two evenings a week at a pace it calls "conversation speed." What this means is that you're supposed to run no faster than the speed at which you can comfortably carry on a conversation with your fellow runners.

Of course, there are other running options if you prefer to break out on your own at your own pace, although congested, high-rise Hong Kong is not one of the world's most runner-friendly cities. One place you might try—one of the few havens of calm in this bustling city—is Victoria Park on Hong Kong Island, overlooking Causeway Bay. The park has a running track as well as other recreational facilities.

One more place to run is Bowen Road, from Stubbs Road (where the Hong Kong Running Clinic is headquartered) to Magazine Gap. The best time of day is early morning, before hyperkinetic Hong Kong cranks into high gear.

Resources
General information: Hong Kong Tourist Association, 548 5th Ave., Suite 590, New York, NY 10036, tel.: 212/869-5008; or 1 Connaught Pl., Hong Kong, tel.: 801-7177.

Route and event information: Hong Kong Running Clinic, 40 Stubbs Rd., Hong Kong, tel.: 574-6211.

Tokyo

Japan is a country in which custom and ritual are given a good deal of respect, something you might want to keep in mind if you plan to run the 3-mile loop around the grounds of the Imperial Palace. The palace is located in the heart of a city that sprawls across hundreds of square miles, and the palace is pretty much the heart of runner's Tokyo.

The proper way to make the run is to begin by warming up in the little courtyard at the Sakuradamon gate. Then proceed counterclockwise, as almost all runners do; to go the other way is very bad, or at least uncustomary, form.

If you're willing to venture out of the city center to run—and to take advantage of broad avenues and open spaces—try Yoyogi-Koen Park or the playing fields of Meiji Jing Outer Gardens. Both will give you an opportunity, if you're so inclined, to take on Tokyo's daunting, though well-marked, subway system. Yes, there are signs in English.

The park is in the Harajuku district (the Yoyogi-Koen stop on the Chiyoda line is your best bet), while the gardens are in the Aoyama district (the subway stop is Gaiemae Station on the Hanzoman or Ginza line).

Resources
General information: Japan National Tourist Organization, 630 5th Ave., Suite 2101, New York, NY 10111, tel.: 212/757-5640. Tourist Information Center, 6-6 Yurakucho, 1 Chome, Chiyoda-ku, Tokyo, tel.: 03/502-1461.

Route and event information: Yomiuri Shimbun, 1-2-1 Kiyosumi, Koto-ku, Tokyo, tel.: 03/242-1111.

EUROPE

Berlin

Do you like your morning run with a taste of recent history thrown in? Head, then, for the Tiergarten, the 630-acre park that begins with the zoo at the eastern end of the Kurfürstendamm, West Berlin's main drag. Beyond the zoo a network of walking paths through the park can be combined to make loops of a mile or more. But here's the historical part: At the park's western extreme is the Brandenburg gate, Berlin's best-known landmark. Pass through or around the gate, past where U.S. TV commentators stood while Germans chiseled away at the Wall; your exact route will depend on how far Berlin has come in its plans to establish a normal flow of pedestrian traffic from west to east. Then onto Unter den Linden, the broad boulevard with wide sidewalks where not long ago helmeted East German soldiers were a more likely sight than runners in singlets.

That's the best route for historically minded runners, and one that's also centrally located. But for the pure experience of a good run—a good, long run—you're better off heading for Grunewald Forest. Within the forest's considerable boundaries, loops of several miles are possible without encountering a car or traffic light. A nice short loop, one on which it's hard to get lost, is around the small lake Grunewaldsee. But because this loop is no more than a mile, you might be inclined to branch out onto one of the many paths that lead from here.

Resources

General information: German Tourist Office, 747 3rd Ave., New York, NY 10017, tel.: 212/308-3300. Verkehrsamt Berlin, Europa Center, Budapeststrasse D-1000 Berlin 30, tel.: 030/262-6031.

Route and event information: SCC Berlin, Meinekestrasse 13, D-1000 Berlin 13, tel.: 882-6405.

London

Could there possibly be a city in the world with more notorious weather than London? Yes, it does rain, but downpours are much rarer than drizzles and periods of lingering dampness—which, as runners know, can actually be pleasant as aerobic activity begins to heat the body. What's more, the fact that summer days are rarely hot and winter days rarely cold can make London's climate something for runners to enjoy, not curse.

London also has several fine places to run. Most centrally located—near a number of major hotels, some of which can provide runners' maps—is the 4-mile loop around Hyde Park and Kensington Garden. The loop can be shortened to 2.5 miles by sticking to the Hyde Park perimeter and cutting across the Serpentine at West Carriage Drive.

For longer runs, Hampstead Heath lies a few miles to the north (if you take the tube, get off at the Hampstead stop). A loop around the edge of the Heath measures almost 7 miles, although shorter routes are possible.

Resources

General information: British Tourist Authority, 40 W. 57th St., New York, NY 10019, tel.: 212/581-4700. City of London Information Centre, St. Paul's Churchyard, London EC4M 8BU, tel.: 071/606-3030.

Route and event information: London Hash House Harriers, 12 Park House Rd., London N11, tel.: 081/361-0887.

Paris

Not long ago, Americans in Paris were easy to spot, at least in the parks; they were the ones running, while natives would be the ones who were strolling. But Parisians in recent years seem to have caught the running bug, and it's easy enough to see why: this is a great city to run in.

The two parks best for running—parks large enough to be called forests—are Bois de Boulogne and Bois de Vincennes. In the former, the premier running spot is the Lac Inférieur, which can be reached via any of three gates: Porte Maillot, Porte Dauphine, or Porte de la Muette. The surface of the 1.65-mile path around the lake is dirt, much like a cross-country trail. Expect company; there are runners here from early morning till early evening. For a longer run, you might prefer the nearly 9-mile loop around the perimeter of Bois de Vincennes. Or if you prefer something shorter and more cultivated, you might try the loop of a little over a mile around Jardin des Tuileries, with its formal gardens and statues.

Paris has a couple of other things going for runners. Winters tend to be mild, and, though summers can be hot, daylight in July and August may extend past 9 PM.

Resources

General information: French Government Tourist Office, 628 5th Ave., New York, NY 10020, tel.: 212/757-1125. Paris Tourist Office, 127 av. des Champs-Elysées, 75008 Paris, tel.: 47-23-61-72.

Route and event information: Fédération Française d'Athlétisme, 10 rue de Faubourg Poissonière, 75010 Paris, tel.: 47-70-90-61. (Ask for the Marche, as in running, department.)

Rome

Rome is a paradox of sorts: It's a city suited to walking but not particularly well suited to running. That is, its narrow back streets are best explored on foot rather than by car or taxi, and, given Rome's renowned traffic congestion, getting from one place to another on foot can be quicker than by car. But the haphazard street layout and the absence of large parks—along with the traffic—make good running routes rare.

In the inner city the place to go is Villa Borghese, the park combining formal gardens, statuary, and museums. A loop of the Pincio Gardens is just .5 mile, but the busts of Italian heros and the view from the Pincio Terrace—across the Piazza del Popolo and the Tiber River—make this run quintessentially Roman, if not aerobically demanding. You can lengthen your Pincio route by heading across the park to the Piazza di Siena, a quarter-mile grass horse track. Longer loops are possible by connecting the various roadways through Villa Borghese. These are generally closed to traffic, but be on the alert nonetheless for the occasional official vehicle.

Another possible place to run is in Janiculum Park, south of the Vatican, Janiculum Hill. But, for the most part, as a runner, you'll probably find Rome frustrating.

Resources

General information: Italian State Tourist Office, 630 5th Ave., New York, NY 10111, tel.: 212/245-4822. EPT (Rome Provincial Tourist Office), Via Parigi 11, Rome 00185, tel.: 06/488-1851.

Route and event information: Consult Runners World *and other running magazines for major events in Rome.*

Zürich

Zürich is one of the world's great banking centers, a title that might imply lots of glass-and-steel architecture and conservatively dressed bankers strolling around with financial secrets concealed in their briefcases. In fact, Zürich is a city of history (dating back more than 2,000 years), sociability (restaurants and hotels abound), and even natural beauty, sitting as it does at the edge of Zürichsee. It is also a city more hospitable to running than the term "banking center" might imply, with several good routes from which to choose. In fact, the banking-center business might work to the advantage of runners, given that finance is a clean industry that produces few lung-clogging pollutants.

If you prefer your running on the flat side, stick to the shores of the Zürichsee. From Bürkliplatz (at the southern end of Bahnhofstrasse, the city's main drag), head in either direction—along the western shore starting at General-Guisan-Quai or across the Quai Bridge to Utoquai along the eastern shore. On both sides you'll find running routes of 1.5 miles along a combination of sidewalks and paved paths.

Resources
General information: Swiss National Tourist Office, 608 5th Ave., New York, NY 10020, tel.: 212/757-5944. Zürich Tourist Office, Bahnhofplatz 15, Zürich, tel.: 01/211-4000.

Route and event information for Switzerland: The World Runners, Hambergersteig 11A, 8008 Zürich, tel.: 01/555-000.

CANADA

Toronto

To suggest that Toronto underwent a renaissance in the '80s could be misleading. That's because "renaissance" implies some sort of rebirth, and many Canadians will argue that, until the '80s, lifeless Toronto had never been born in the first place.

Today the general Canadian consensus is that Toronto has at last come of age as a center of finance, communication, and transportation. Nevertheless, a couple of the elements that might be traced to its stodgy, conservative past—cleanliness and safety—remain in place, for which runners can be thankful.

What's more, Toronto has plenty of good running routes. The Toronto Islands—a 550-acre, car-free park comprising four islands in Lake Ontario—is one of the neater places to run. Start with the 1.5-mile boardwalk from Centre Island to Ward's Island. From here you can lengthen your route by connecting with the paths that run along the beaches of Ward Island. The drawbacks are the breezes (which, although pleasantly cooling in summer, can be bone-chilling at other times of year) and the eight-minute ferry ride (leaving the harbor from behind the Harbour Castle Westin) required to get to the islands.

If you're looking for an alternative route, the Martin Goodman Trail runs along the waterfront for 12 miles from the Balmy Beach Club in the east end to the beaches southwest of High Park.

Resources
General information: Metropolitan Toronto Convention and Visitors Association, 207 Queen's Quay W, Suite 509, Toronto, ON M5J LA7, tel.: 416/368-9821. Ontario Travel, Queens Park, Toronto, ON M7A 2E5, tel.: 416/965-4008.

Route and event information: Metro Parks Department, Toronto, tel.: 416/392 8186.

AUSTRALIA

Sydney

Much of Sydney might remind a U.S. visitor of Los Angeles. The urban sprawl reaches far inland, and a temperate climate gives the city a decidedly southern-Californian character. But harborside Sydney is a high-rise business district along a shoreline indented with bays and coves.

This layout does not necessarily make for great running. However, there is one good downtown route, one that may be populated in the middle of the day with office workers out for a lunch-hour run. The route begins at Circular Quay, passes by the Opera House—the winged sail structure that is Sydney's most recognizable landmark—then bends through the Royal Botanic Gardens before finishing on Macquarie Street. In all, a run of a little less than a mile.

If you happen to be in the eastern suburbs, you might want to try the marked route that runs south along the cliffs from Bondi Beach. There are distance markers as well as exercise stations along the way.

Resources

General information: Australian Tourist Commission, 2121 Ave. of the Stars, Suite 1200, Los Angeles, CA 90067, tel.: 213/552-1988. Travel Centre of New South Wales, 19 Castlereagh St., Sydney, New South Wales 2000, tel.: 02/231-4444.

Route and event information: Australian Runner Magazine, Box 396, Malvern, Victoria 3141, tel.: 03/819-9225.